YOUNG WRITERS

OVER THE MOON

STAFFORDSHIRE

Published in Great Britain in 1997 by
POETRY NOW
1-2 Wainman Road, Woodston,
Peterborough, PE2 7BU

HB ISBN 1 86188 117 7
SB ISBN 1 86188 112 6

Foreword

The *Over The Moon* competition was an overwhelming success - over 43,000 entries were received from 8-11 year olds up and down the country, all written on a wide variety of subjects. Reading all these poems has been a painstaking task - but very enjoyable.

Many of the poems were beautifully illustrated. This just emphasises how much time, effort and thought was put into the work. For me, this makes the editing process so much harder.

I hope that *Over The Moon Staffordshire* highlights the diversity of today's young minds. I believe that each of these poems shows a great deal of creativity and imagination. Many of them also express an understanding of the problems, socially and environmentally, that we are all facing.

The poems that follow are all written on different levels, and some are more light-hearted than others. With a considerable variety of subjects and styles, there should be something to appeal to everyone.

Sarah Andrew
Editor

CONTENTS

Rebecca Eady	19
Jenny Cozens	19
Elicia Cooke	20
Simon Oliver	20
Thomas Bloor	21
George Barlow	21
Katrina Boardman	22
Emma Ruth Taylor	22
Rose Allen	23
Thomas McMeekin	23
Kirsty Hood	24
Rebecca Brough	24
Jonathan Eady	25
Lucy Marsh	25
Gabriel Mulenga	26
Benjamin Byatt	26
Daniel Jones	27
Stacey Alcock	27
Sara Swindells	27
Ben Keay	28
Georgina Winczaryk	28
Chantelle Hillman	29
Carl Hales	29
Joanne Parsons	30
Alex Shaughnessy	30
Sophia Khalid	30
Matthew Dalgarno	31
Steven Walklate	32

Hillside Primary School

Sarah Woodward	32
Elizabeth Cooper	33
Kimberley Perry	34
Victoria Cooper	35

Holy Rosary Primary School

Sophie Farrell	35
Sian Desay	36
Lara Desay	36
Nicola Stanbridge	37

John Bamford Primary School

Nicola Bailey	37
Nicola Rogers &	
Gemma Price	38
Matthew McElroy	38
Jamie Herbert	39
Jamie Baker	39
Danielle Spence	40
Scott Eccleshall	40
Adam Seager	41
Robert O'Gorman	41

Landywood Primary School

Nicholas Russell	42
Laura Edwards	42
Gemma Allcock	43
Sam Card	43

Newstead Primary School

Kayleigh Cornes	44
Phillip Marsh	44
Claire Walford	45
Liam Johnson	45
Lesley Mountford	46
Nicola Edwards	46
Richard Whitehurst	47
Kayleigh Bird	47
Kimberley Dutton	48
Natasha Baddeley	48

Norton Canes Primary School

Grace Hutchinson	48
Kelly Cadman	49
Jenna Claye	49
James Whittaker	50
Rebecca Bate	50
Carly Simpson	51
David McCracken	51
Emma Wallage	52
Lee Prince	52

St Chad's Primary School, Lichfield

St Dominic's Priory School, Stone

Emma Tonks	77
Katherine Shanahan	70
Fiona James	70
Rosanna Jones	71
Ellie Davies	71
Lauren Tompkinson	72
Rebecca Thomas	72
Helena Somervail	73
Ffion Carlin	73
Davina Charlton	74
Philip Edwards	74
Kimberley Addison	75
Andrew Flather	75
Rebecca Ford	76
Kelly Holland	76
Rhiannon Caudwell	77
Jodi Bradbury	77
Katie Adamson	78
Zoe Maiden	78
Gemma Brunt	79
Charlie Cooper	79
Georgina Frieder	80
Harriet Bell	80
Sarah Passmore	81
Samantha Jones	81
Rebecca Holmes	82
Amy Baker	83
Amy Sanders	83
Teresa Fitzherbert	84
Sophie Ryan	84
Tamsin Sawyer	85
Katie Gough	85
Alexandra Evans	86
Abigail Frankish	86
Lydia Austen	87
Charlotte Heywood	87
Elizabeth Evans	88

St Elizabeth RC Primary School

Len Wright	88
Rachel Brownsword	89
Mark Roberts	90
Ruth Baldwin	90
Lauren Holden	91
Matthew Henson	92
Charlene Baker	93
Daniel Clark	93
Dannielle Appleby	94
Alex Henson	95
Matthew Atkins	96
Amy Cole	96
John Connor	97
Jamie Sidaway	98
Ruth Jordan	99
Ben Wilkins	100

St John's CE Primary School

Thomas Halsted	100
Rebecca Davies-Thomas	101
Davis Travis	101
Bradley Tooley	102
Marc Malloy	102

St Mary's RC Primary School, Cannock

Rebecca Langley	103
Thomas Muller	103
Sarah Davison	104
Carly Wall	104
Samantha Jackson	105
Stuart France	105
Daniel Taylor	106
Sara Reynolds	106
Harriet Beeston	107
Thomas Lyonette	107
Katie Smythies	108

St Michael's School, Lichfield

Sarah Carter	108
Stephen Darby	109

The Close Junior School

Elizabeth Williamson	127
Jessica Stephenson	128

The Faber RC Primary School

Alicia Hibberts	128
Vanessa Rowlinson	129
Thomas Shenton	130
James Hall	130
Thomas Bishop	131
Victoria Brindley	131
Rosanna Rowlinson	132
Lorna Gould	132

Park Primary School

Samantha Hatton	133
Natalie Arrowsmith	133
Amy Langford	134
Emma Rigby	134
Lindsey Pullin	135
Victoria Pople	135
Caroline Wall	136
Matthew Lloyd	136
Heidi Thacker	136
Nicola Williams	137
Hannah Spencer	137
Nicola Pegg	138
Daniel Warner	138
Nicholas Gregory	138
Dominic Pitt	139
Craig Ball	139
Paul Brookes	140
Michael Rigby	140
Neil Birch	141
Ashley Lawton	141

Walhouse CE Junior School

Hayley Stanton	142
Christian Bury	142
Richard Meads	142
Oliver Lawton Poxon	143

THE PAINT BOX

I had a paint box yesterday
From it I had joy and play
The colours they weren't too bright
But each glowed with delight

I had no red for wounds or blood
I had no brown for dirt or mud
I had no yellow for the burning sands
I had no black for an orphan child in a foreign land

Instead I had
Orange for joy and life
I had a blue for a clear blue sky
I had pink for the truth, no lie
So I sat down with these colours
Out of the way of others
And painted
Peace

Vicki Wootton (11) Brindley Heath Junior School

HAIKU

Winter . . .
Clear heavens open,
Silver snowflakes softly fall,
Branches hang lifeless.

Spring . . .
Flowers graze in fields,
Silver clouds float through clear skies,
Nature life begins.

Summer . . .
Golden sun shines bright,
A burning fire gleams above,
Lawns of laughing youths.

Autumn . . .
A mad wind rages,
Lifting gold, amber leaves,
Sandy bronze bark flakes

Hannah Smith (11) Brindley Heath Junior School

THE CREATION (A VIKING LEGEND)

In the middle there was Gingaugap;
Nothingness, emptiness, void, non existence;

To the north there was ice;
It was gelid, a huge open freezer, frost bound;
A rigid-climate, frozen over, like a colossal see through blanket;
Bleak, Siberian temperatures, bitter cold;

In the southern region it was quite different;
Fire, searing heat, black smoke rising;
A combustion, blistering hot, a huge flaring inferno;

The regions met;
The flames melting the ice, slush oozing to the ground;

Out of the thaw emerged Hymeir an evil
Frost giant, the first living creature the world had seen.

Richard Campbell (11) Brindley Heath Junior School

MY BADMINTON CLUB

Tuesday; I'm going to badminton club on Thursday
        I've never been before I've started to feel a
        bit weird now got to go 'cause I've
        bought my form.

Wednesday; I feel as though every one's going to
        laugh at me because I don't know how
        to play. I wish I wasn't going now 'cause
        I've got tummy ache.

Thursday night; My badminton club is now over it
        wasn't so bad after all nobody even looked
        at me even when I dropped the ball.

Lisa Hughes (11) Chesterton Primary School

MY LIFE AT SCHOOL

My belly is big
My bottom is small
My thighs are enormous
And I'm not very tall

I haven't any friends
They all call me blob
It makes me so upset
That I begin to sob

They all say that I'm ugly
I wonder if it's true
But when they start to pick on me
I say you wouldn't like it if it was you

But then they get angry
And my face turns bright red
I free myself and runaway
But they throw stones at my head

Then I tell the teacher
She tells them one by one
All of you, you're expelled
So now they all are gone

Our school isn't very big
If you come you'll see
There's lots and lots of teachers
But the only pupil is me

Steven West (11) Chesterton Primary School

4

FAVOURITE DOLLS

My favourite dolls
My favourite dolls
So many what will I do
White dolls, brown dolls
Spotted dolls long haired short haired dolls
So many what will I do
I do not know what to do

My favourite dolls
I play with them a lot
I hug them in bed
My cousins play with them
My hair style doll
I play with her a lot
So many what will I do

My favourite dolls
Do you know what I can do
I hope you can help me?
Please help, please help, oh please help
So many, so many, oh no, so many
Please help, oh please help me
So many, many, many.

Amy Dunthorne (10) Chesterton Primary School

TAKE CARE

Please don't smoke
It makes me choke.

Don't take drugs
They are for thugs.

Please stop and think
Before you drink.

Last of all, don't talk to strangers.
Please beware of all these dangers.

Naomi Waters (11) English Martyr's RC (A) Primary School

THE OLD LADY

She sat alone and thought
About the good and sad.
Old as she was
She could remember
All the times she'd had.
Her old eyes showed
How upset she was
With no more friends or family.
It has been like this for thirty years
'How my laughs have turned into tears'

Ann Marie Flatley (11) English Martyr's RC (A) Primary School

THE SEA

Look at the sea
The foam is a beautiful lady's hair
Her cold dress
Is the silk waves
There are stranger visions
That are not really there
The deepest part
Is her deep blue eyes

Listen to the sea
In her bad mood
Her voice is cold and evil
The strange visions
Are now devils
But once again
Her dress goes silky

Touch the sea
Her skin is silky
Her hair tickles your fingers
But her dress is cold

Smell the sea
She has a deep aroma
Just smelling her
You know she is cold and silky

Taste the sea
Her hair is bitter
And so is her dress

Charlotte Rollin (8) Etching Hill Primary School

I LIKE THE SUN

I like the sun glittering and shining
In the sparkling blue sky
The birds flying in the blue warm hot
Sun
The sun is hot the sun sparkles like
Glitter in the blue blooming sky I love
The cold water on my hot tiny face.

How I love the sun.

Kelly Johnson (8) Greenways School

THE STORM ON THE BEACH

The thunder rolling in the sky,
The lightning splitting it up.
The waves are lashing against the rocks,
Like the smashing of a cup.

The rain is falling in torrents,
Like water from the devil.
The lightning flashed across the sky,
The thunder rolled like evil.

The waves are bellowing and roaring,
Like an angry lion in a cage.
The thunder's growling in the clouds,
Like a giant in a rage.

And now the storm has died away,
No more clapping or growling.
The storm has gone to another land,
After the storm the calm.

Nicola Amos (9) Greenways School

THE THINGS I LOVE

Meadows covered in gleaming daffodils,
Kittens purring outside the door,
The blazing fire keeping me warm,
The freezing snow freezes up my feet.

Rain stinging my face all over,
Tea, warm tea warms me up
Fire, warm blazing fire heating from the coal,
Trees autumn leaves are falling off onto the floor.

Wind, pushing and forging past,
Leaves, covering up trees and places,
Grass, covering soil and fields,
Water, cold and warm keeping me warm and hot.

Lauren Rae Cole (8) Greenways School

THESE THINGS I LIKE

I like the stinging
From the cold frozen rain
The blazing hot sun
When I just come out to play.

I like it when I look
Through my black binoculars
In my house
I see all kinds of birds.

I like it when I'm sitting
Right by the fire
Just when I come out
Of my shower.

Ben Watkins (8) Greenways School

A GRASS POEM

In the morning the grass flows
Covered with sheen
All a-glowing
Where the grass is green

In the afternoon all dry and wavy
The grass is still there
Out of motion
And taking care

In the evening the grass grows short
I'm looking down from the port
Grass has green blades growing from the ground
When I look I see what I've found

In the night it is very dark
But there are still cars in the park
Suddenly it goes very bright
And the grass goes very tight

Jessica L Rees (8) Greenways School

THESE THINGS I LOVE

I love the sound of the tweeting
Birds in the morning.
And the cat as it purrs
When you stroke him.
And the cows they chase each
Other in their fields.
And the fresh grass sitting on
The ground.
And I love the little bugs on
The window.

Samantha Foster (8) Greenways School

UNDER THE SEA

Under the sea down deep comes a shark with sharp
teeth.
Trout in the stream jumping high supreme like a dream
Salmon big fat juicy all around
Octopus's legs wrapping round a fish opening its jaws ready
For lunch.

Kristian Clarke (8) Greenways School

THESE THINGS I LOVE

These I have loved - fresh clean water
Flowing down the stream and
The light of the sun at
Dawn

I love to see the lambs up
On the hilltop eating the grass
Below them and to hear the
Birds singing happily in the
Summer breeze.

I love to watch the little
Ladybirds crawling up my arm
And to see the squirrels climbing
Down to get all of the chestnuts
Below them.

I love to hear the waterfall
Playing its beautiful notes and
To smell the turkey cooking so
Nicely.

I love to see the bright flowers
Growing so fast and the trees
Giving me shade

Amy Walthall (8) Greenways School

11

THINGS I LOVE

Lovely kittens going in and out of my legs
The blazing sun on my face
The freezing cold snow on Christmas day.
The tweeting birds on the trees in the blazing sunlight
The green grass sitting on the ground lovely to see
The lovely horses walking on the ground of grass
The lovely wind in the night, lovely that is.

Kiki Pilarczyk (8) Greenways School

THESE THINGS I LOVE

I love the fragrance
Of flowers in my garden,
I love the gleaming sun
In the sky,
I love to go and ride
My bike,
I love the singing of the
Birds in the day time,
I love the taste of boiling hot tea,
I love the fresh cut grass
In the meadow field,
I love to sit by the fire
On a cold and chill day.

I love the softness of the fluffy towels
When I get out of the bath,
I love the soft snow,
Landing on my face,
I love to go to play
In the snow,
I love to go sledging
In the snow.

Mathew Sampson (8) Greenways School

12

THESE THINGS I LOVE

Fresh leaves hanging on the tall brown trees.
The smell of the flowers waving from the gloomily wind.
I came in from a winter night and smell the shining hot fire.
I love the sound of the joyful birds singing on the hillside.
I love the messing with my hair after a refreshing bath.
I love to watch the light brown squirrels running up the tree.
I love to watch the ladybirds crawling
on the ground with their wings showing
and ready to fly.
I love to see my friend's cats playing
with the twigs or a branch.
I love to see that my Nanny's dog is
Enjoying herself and playing with her squeaky
Toys.
I love to see those bright faces,
In the classroom,
And working very peacefully.

Gemma Clow (8) Greenways School

I LIKE ...

The sea was swaying side to side
Hitting all the boats nearby
We all go down to see
Such things we almost never knew
Like galloping horses running
Through the woods and the sea
Swishing against the boat.
The stars and love is bright.

Charlotte Barrow (7) Greenways School

13

THESE THINGS I ADORE

Beautiful trees with shining glossy leaves,
Soft towels after a hot bath,
Delightful yellow meadows blowing in the
Soft wind,
Lots of little flowers dancing in the
Sun.

Boats slowing peacefully along a river,
Little kittens playing with balls of cotton wool,
Little rain drops shining in the sun,
Beautiful blossoms blooming in the white mist.
Cold wind blowing on the waving trees,
Men and women laughing at night,
Little spotty ladybirds crawling about in the sun,
The big waves slashing in the wind,
Flower petals swirling about in the wind.

Emily Lydia Wright (8) Greenways School

THESE THINGS I LOVE

Water splashing on my hands
Grass twitching on my hands.
The wind rustling leaves and rainbows
Swans and ducks quacking
Ladybirds crawling on my fingers
Trees shade me in the sun
When I go to school

Gary Watwood (8) Greenways School

THESE THINGS I LOVE

Towels are soft after a hot bath,
Kittens rolling in cotton wool,
Buttercups gleaming in spring meadows
Rain pattering the windows.

Interesting stories sitting by the fire,
Birds singing in tree tops,
Hair fragrance like flowers,
Boats flowing peacefully.

Autumn leaves falling from tree tops,
Blossom trees blooming in sunlight,
The raindrops biting my bitter face,
Minute ladybirds crawling up my back.

Snow tickling my face,
Trees blowing in the breeze,
The water in the sea splashing,
Sunshine shining on houses.

Tina Sanzeri (8) Greenways School

ELEPHANTS

Fat grey elephants strong, powerful
Also gentle and stamping around
Chewing leaves off the trees
Rolling around in dirty mud
Squirting water out of their trunks
Eating and sleeping all day long
Danger is coming poached for
Their ivory.
            Save the elephants!

Alex Lister (10) Harpfield CP School

15

PANDAS

Pandas eat, pandas sleep
They're always a popular attraction in zoos
They're furry, they're soft, they're loveable, cuddly and funny too!
I wonder why they're black and white?
Their big gentle eyes make them look so cute
They have black fur around their legs
I wonder why they're black and white?
They must support Port Vale
But I still don't know why they're black and white!

Sarah Taylor (11) Harpfield CP School

THE ELEPHANT

The elephant is bold and strong
Stamping feet in every stride
Eating leaves, fruit and tree bark
     Big grey lumbering giant
Poached for ivory
Strong
Rare
     Big grey lumbering giant
Eating and sleeping all day
Wanted for jewellery
Creamy tusks
     Big grey lumbering giant
Their trunks are strong and wide
Numbers are growing fewer
Danger is coming
     Big grey lumbering giant
     Save the elephants

Gemma Larkin (11) Harpfield CP School

MY GRAN

My little old gran is kind, and generous to me,
But she lives in Scotland, so I don't see her much.
She doesn't live far away from my lively aunty
And my loud cousin,
When we stay, I sleep in her room.
She reminds me of the colour red, because she's
Warm and kind, and she always wears it,
She lets me do almost anything.
But I wish she could do it with me,
I hope she comes to see us soon,
Because Scotland is so far away.

Laura Bettaney (11) Harpfield CP School

POLLUTION

Black dust swirling over my head,
I feel sick,
The sea filled with thick black oil,
Birds floating in oily pools
On top of the water,
Factories and cars,
Belching smoke and pollution,
Clouds heavy with poison,
Cruel killing pine forests,
I can hear the acid,
Dripping into the still air,
Gases mixing together,
To form a death cocktail,
Make it stop,
Please make it stop.

Jessica Street (11) Harpfield CP School

MY SISTER

She's green always on
The go
She's like a lion
She rips me apart
With her long sharp
Nails,
Smart chic always
The latest gear,
Moans and groans
About her food
Enthusiastically dancing
All day long and all
Night too.
She ought to be
A teacher she bosses
So much
I hopefully wish
She was smaller
Then I could boss
Her.

Paul Hinchley (11) Harpfield CP School

ANIMALS

Animals, animals grow so fast.
There's giraffes and elephants
Grow so big. There are birds
That can fly in the air.
That swoop and dive in the air.
And animals in the water swim
Underneath the ocean.
Where it is dark and quiet.

Adam Taylor (8) Harpfield CP School

18

BLACK AND WHITE

Black and white
They live in the misty mountains of China
Munching through tall bamboo shoots
Spending 12 hours eating
Every day
Black and white
They're killed for their skins
They are a symbol of the WWF
They look very big and cuddly
Black and white
They're kept in zoos to try and breed them
Giant pandas are very rare
Black and white
Save the Panda

Rebecca Eady (11) Harpfield CP School

THE KILLER WHALE

The blazing sunset shining red
Shines down on the darkening sea
A black dorsal fin knifes the surface
Of the water mother leading the way
And another fin
I think it's amazing breath-taking
Whales racing though the flowing sun
Set sea. Grabbing a fish she dives
Down deep to the depth of the sea.
Followed by her family.

Jenny Cozens (11) Harpfield CP School

THE WHALE

It's not fair,
The whale the gentle giant swims so quietly,
It's not fair,
Hunted unaware of danger,
Speaking a mysterious language we don't understand,
Maybe one day in the future we will,
It's not fair,
They never harmed us in any way,
Maybe sometime in life we will leave them alone,
It's not fair,
That their numbers should go down down down,
It's not fair.

Elicia Cooke (11) Harpfield CP School

TADPOLES

Tadpoles, tadpoles swimming in a pond
Growing back legs growing front legs
Black all over
Got a little tail
Stick to plants
Come out of jelly eggs
The tail disappears into a lump
Grows a bit bigger
And then it is a frog.

Simon Oliver (8) Harpfield CP School

ANIMALS

Some animals are cute like furry fluffy puppies.
Some animals are vicious like tigers, lions and bears.
Some have beaks short and long.
Sharks are vicious they eat fish.
Some fish have gills and others haven't.
Snakes are slimy and slithery
A giraffe has a long neck so they can eat leaves off the trees.
They are very spotty
Horses gallop, trot and run,
There are all sorts of the animals in the world.

Thomas Bloor (8) Harpfield CP School

TADPOLES

Tadpoles, tadpoles swimming in a pond.
Sucking on weeds, back legs growing.
Eating each other, front legs growing.
Little black dots swimming very fast.
With their tiny tails that move from right to left.
Born from little jelly kind of eggs.
Then turns into a *frog* at last.

George Barlow (8) Harpfield CP School

I LIE IN A MEADOW

I lie in a meadow under the sky,
Clouds pass, pass me by.
I lie in the grass the long green grass
I lie under they blow they blow
I lie under a windy tree it blows
And it blows
I lie on a hill next to flowers, flowers blow.

Katrina Boardman (8) Harpfield CP School

MY LAUGHING GRANDAD

My laughing grandad is called Ron
He takes tablets but we don't know what they are
We are sure they are laughing tablets
He is so fat and it's lucky that he can fit through the front door
When he is laughing because he laughs so much
That he is nearly on the floor outside the front door.
He eats so much that he nearly burst one day
In the pub
He is so fat that one day in the pub, when
He got up off his seat his trousers fell down
He was laughing so much that we could
Not stop him
We'll get him a red suit
My own jolly Santa Claus.

Emma Ruth Taylor (11) Harpfield CP School

BREAKFAST TIME

Sizzling sausages in the pan.
Tossing pancakes in the air.
Toast in the toaster popping up and down.
Bacon under the grill cooking well.
Beans in the can ready to be cooked.
Salt and pepper sprinkled on top.
Brown sauce at the side.
Yum yum nice food on my plate.

Rose Allen (7) Harpfield CP School

FOOTBALL

Football is good but you get
covered in mud.

Football strips always get ripped.

Football is ace but you get
hit in the face.

The goalie is good but he gets
the most mud.

You can tackle and you can hurt
your ankle.

Thomas McMeekin (8) Harpfield CP School

MY HOUSE

H is for house the best place to be
O is for orange nice and tasty
U is for an ugly brother
S is for snug when I'm in bed
E is for an enjoyable house.

Oh I wish I could stay in
my lovely house!

Kirsty Hood (8) Harpfield CP School

MICHELLE

Michelle is a grumpy old soul,
A quick black cloud of moods over her head,
When she gets tired of work,
She goes to the sink,
And busily washes up the glue cups,
She regularly plays noughts and crosses.
She likes to get her own way.
Or she will be in a mood all day,
She looks like a panda,
With huge black eyes,
And short dark hair.
She owns a cat
She always chats about,
Clowy the cat,
Michelle is a pale girl,
And likes to eat slimy spaghetti,
She hates to wear school ties,
She wishes to have a room of her own.

Rebecca Brough (10) Harpfield CP School

THE VERY TIDY HOUSE

Everything is clean in the very tidy house,
Even in the garden lives a very tidy mouse,
It's as clean as a pin,
Even in the biscuit tin,
No crumbs on the floor,
No marks on the door,
Outside, the flowerbeds are very, very neat.
Even looking at the garden is a very special treat.

Jonathan Eady (8) Harpfield CP School

HARTSHILL

Harpfield, Harpfield,
in Hartshill.
Ambulance rushes
past the bus stop,
church and dinner centre
with an emergency.
The milkman passes.

The ice-cream man
passed the newsagents
passed Quarry Road and back.

Fire bell rings at the school.
The fire engine rushes to the school,
stops at the gates as it picks up the injured.
Waves to the teacher in the yard.
Straight to the unit and straight to the
X-ray and straight back home!

Lucy Marsh (8) Harpfield CP School

ON MY WAY TO CHURCH

I go to the bus stop, on my way to church.
And suddenly I saw the ambulance
swerve round the bend.

It went past the dinner centre,
it went past the late shop,
it swerved past Victoria Street.

And at last the bus came
and the driver was a pain,
so I got the bus and started again.

Gabriel Mulenga (8) Harpfield CP School

WE LIVE HERE

We live here.
It is a very
nice place.
We put the litter
in the bins.
We don't kill animals,
here oh no.
We live our world
it is great.
I've got some friends.
I go to school it is
very good.

Benjamin Byatt (8) Harpfield CP School

POETRY

Jobs, jobs why are there jobs.
Jobs for adults,
School for children
Lots of work for us.
And lots of work for adults.

Daniel Jones (9) Harpfield CP School

SPLISH, SPLASH

Splish, splash, bang, crash in the forest in the pan
Once or twice squash and squeeze
It drips down your chin with ease
You drink it too and you drink it all the time
It is water, yes it's water
You have it in your fruit
I've told you what it is
It's water.

Stacey Alcock (7) Harpfield Cp School

SLITHERY SLUGS

Slugs slither along the soil
Leaving a trail behind them
Under the stones is where they live.
Gobbling the vegetables
Slimy slugs eat the plants.

Sara Swindells (8) Harpfield CP School

VERY FUNNY JON

Jon is my best friend,
He has short, brown and straight hair,
He is very, very funny!
Jon is tall with long legs,
He plays football quite skilfully,
I think he will make a good giraffe,
With those long legs of his,
I wish I will still be his friend in
10 years time,
I would be devastated if I lost him
As a friend.

Ben Keay (11) Harpfield CP School

WATER

Water is in the sky
Water is in the tap
Water is in the sea
We need water to help us to live
The plants need water
We need water
The animals need water
The people on our hill
The trees need water
The frogs need water
The world needs water.

Georgina Winczaryk (8) Harpfield CP School

HARTSHILL

Hartshill, Hartshill, every day.
At Hartshill
School.
In Hartshill
Church.
In Hartshill you can
hear the bells
ringing,
and ringing
all day long.
You can
hear the milkman,
early in the morning.
You can hear the ambulance
going by, with
people in
who are
ill.

Chantelle Hillman (9) Harpfield CP School

A HOUSE

I live in a house
In Stoke-on-Trent
It is very smelly
But I want to go
Somewhere else
But the world is nice
But where can you hide.

Carl Hales (8) Harpfield CP School

SWIMMING

I love to go in the bath
And I like to go in the swimming pool
I like to splash my friends
And I love to go down the slide
And I end up all wet
And I think swimming is good fun.

Joanne Parsons (8) Harpfield CP School

MY DOG

My small, silly, black and white dog
He barks loudly at anything that moves
He loves playing with tennis balls
He loves to run wild everywhere
He always wags his small tail
He is very, very silly
But he's my silly, small, black and
White dog.

Alex Shaughnessy (11) Harpfield CP School

SPLISH, SPLASH

Splish, splash in my bath
Splish, splash on the tap
Splish, splash on my head
Where has the water come from
Outside it's the rain.

Sophia Khalid (8) Harpfield CP School

HARTSHILL

The ambulance is noisy all day.
The bus stop is crowded with people.
On Sundays the church bell goes
Ding dong.
At dinner time the centre is dirty.
If you are ill you need an emergency.
The fire bell
is precious.
In the gateway you will
meet someone at
the door.
Hartshill is a place.
Ice-cream is delicious to eat.
Jobs can be hard to earn.
Bottle kilns are smoky.
We get food from the late shop.
Milkmen are early in the morning.
Newsagents have the news we want.
Optician checks your eyes.
Palmers Green is a road.
We queue up for things.
Railings stop you breaking in.
Schools are where we learn.
We learn from the teachers.
The accident unit is where we get better.
Victoria Street is very long.
Walls are very hard.
We X-ray our bones.
Yards are full of people.
The zebra-crossing helps us cross a road.

Matthew Dalgarno (9) Harpfield CP School

RICHARD

Richard is my best friend
He laughs like a hyena
And is as tall as a giraffe
He supports Stoke and
Likes football
He's got a SNES like me
He plays games with me
As well.

Steven Walklate (11) Harpfield CP School

FIRE

Fire crackling, blazing fire.
It's hot and smoky, bubbly and red.
Rising higher and higher.
Engulfing all that's around it.

Fire exploding like a flaming volcano.
Red, yellow, orange, blowing with a sigh.
Like a colourful bird taking off to fly,
Fire climbing way up high.

Out goes the fire.
Cooling down with the fireman's hose.
How it started nobody knows,
There's no more fire.

Out goes the fire.
All you can see is the black burnt-out
Old church spire.
No more flames of fire.
No more flames rising higher and higher.

Sarah Woodward (9) Hillside Primary School

PE

'It's PE today!' said Fay,
'Oh no!' groaned Joe.
Children cheered everywhere
Children jumping in the air.
'Come around, come around.'
Shouted Mrs Fall.
'You're going to fall Paul.'
I did skipping while the teacher was
Flipping, (with Paul).
In the race I came 1st!
While Sarah was drinking some
Fruit burst.
But what is the worst
Is in the sack!
Sarah was giving Katie
A piggyback!
'PE can be fun!'
Cried my mum's best friend's son.
In long jump I got 2m 23cm . . .
            Did you see?
Oliver won the race!
Then I saw Mrs Fall's face,
Burning up as bright as the sun.
(I don't think she was having fun!)
Lydia fell then went the bell.

Elizabeth Cooper (10) Hillside Primary School

THE WIND IN THE TREES

Hustling, bustling through the silver birch,
Quickly racing the falling leaves to the ground.
Back up he races.
But now he whistles on.
On to the mighty oak
Trying to tear away the leaves
The oak clings onto its green.
The great north wind moves onto the ash tree.
In one blow the leaves were gone.
It looked like it was *shivering*.
The leaves spread far and wide.
He whistles on.
He goes to the cherry blossom.
He dare not blow her blossom away!
Past he goes quietly creeping,
Onto the conker tree.
Wildly tossing its branches around high in the sky.
Conkers come down to the ground
Clattering, crunching.
The wind seems to rest on the autumn leaves.
In the morning the wind goes past the cherry blossom,
But blows her blossom away!
She dips and sways madly
But soon night comes and the wind rests.

Kimberley Perry (10) Hillside Primary School

LISTEN!

Why don't people listen?
Why don't they care?
Are they deaf or something?
As if I'm not there!
They put their arm around me
And say 'Go over there.'
Or they don't hear my voice.
I am part of this world!
I am really here!

Victoria Cooper (10) Hillside Primary School

THE BECKONING SEA

I love the sea, the beautiful sea,
With its beckoning song to come,
The gulls that cry, waiting for food,
And the crash of the open sea.

I like the sea, the beautiful sea,
And its jumping and springing dance.
The fish below, all swimming away,
With their shimmering tails in the sun.

I love the sea, the beautiful sea,
With its timeless and carefree tide.
I love the wind, the whistling wind,
And its running and swirling way.

I like the sea, the beautiful sea,
And its mixing and moving way.
I love the water, the cold water
And the beautiful coastline shores.

Sophie Farrell (11) Holy Rosary Primary School

SPRING

Flowers are budding everywhere,
Petals are blowing here and there.

Sun shining in the sky,
Lovely time to bake a pie.

Everyone is having fun,
Would you like a cream bun.

Leaves are forming on the trees,
Starting to hear the buzzing of bees.

Sian Desay (10) Holy Rosary Primary School

DELIGHT

I walked in the forest one day.
Through the oak and sycamore trees.
The rustling leaves and crackling acorns.
It's a real delight for me.

> I walked past a lake one day
> And I gazed at the pouncing fish.
> I walked on the wet muddy ground.
> It's a real delight for me.

I walked along the countryside one day.
And observed the pastures and fields.
I looked at the different types of flowers,
It's a real delight for me.

> I walked along the beach one day,
> And admired the immeasurable sea,
> I watched the boats sail away,
> It's a real delight for me.

Lara Desay (11) Holy Rosary Primary School

SEA AND STORM

Sea mingles with sand
hauling debris from on shore,
Strange objects tangle in its swirl,
Foamy curls dash the rocks,
The storm shatters the silence,
Lightning flashes, thunder claps,
The water tosses to and fro,
Waves collide, splashing crazily.
Suddenly, stillness comes,
The waves die down,
Sun, with radiant colour
Lights the sky,
The storm, has ended.

Nicola Stanbridge (11) Holy Rosary Primary School

DAFFODIL

Look there's Daffodil laughing with his mates,
What's the joke I wonder?
Is he laughing at me?

Ha ha laughs Daffodil again,
I wish I was in the picture,
Oh what can he be laughing at?

Now he's calling his mates over,
I'm getting restless,
Why can't he just go away?

He's just being silly,
I'm taking no notice,
I walk straight past the laughing man,
With my head in the air,
For my name is Tulip!

Nicola Bailey (9) John Bamford Primary School

TULIP

Look at the proud tulip in his new suit,
Just bought it from the tailors you know.
How happy he seems as he strolls down the street,
With his suitcase and umbrella in his hand!

Handsome young fellow, looks lovely in red,
Say the old ladies in the bank,
Wonder where he got that top from, they say
My husband would love one of them.

As he walks home through the street,
Feeling very tired and exhausted,
Dragging his feet along the floor,
Can't wait to be home again.

When he gets home he drops his things on the floor
Sits on the settee and watches TV.
At ten o'clock he goes to bed,
Goodnight, he says, goodnight.

Nicola Rogers (10) & Gemma Price (11) John Bamford Primary School

THE DAISY

Daisy is nice, kind and friendly lying in a
field of green all day.
Daisy likes playing with the others
in the field all day long.
Daisy likes playing ballerinas
in the shining sun.
Daisy is white, golden inside,
she glistens in the sun as she plays.
Daisy is cheerful all day long singing
merrily to a song.

Matthew McElroy (11) John Bamford Primary School

ROSE THE POEM

Look out
There goes a chair,
Everyone ducks
As it flies through the air.

Shouting at the children
She never ever stops,
Then one child shouts
Let's call the cops.

That's the way
To describe the rose,
Short tempered, very irritable,
I suppose, that's the way it goes.

On the other hand
She's really into romance,
You just watch her
Having a smoochy dance.

Jamie Herbert (11) John Bamford Primary School

DANDELION

Standing, proudly amongst the grass,
The bright dandelion looking its best,
Everyone puts him to the test,
They tell him to run they tell him to fly,
In the end he never loses.
The dandelion is good at hiding,
Because at night he closes up,
If you speak to him he will cheer you up,
He is cool just have a look.

Jamie Baker (11) John Bamford Primary School

HERE IS THE TULIP AGAIN

Here is the tulip again,
Looking very smart,
Very proud and very posh,
Dozing in the sun.

Here is the tulip again,
Head high in the air,
Listening to the music,
In the busy bank.

Here is the tulip again,
Dressed up in a skirt,
Starts to do some dancing,
Instead of doing work.

Danielle Spence (11) John Bamford Primary School

SUNFLOWER

Proudly the sunflower worships the sun,
With her bright yellow petals sticking out.
She lounges around by the pool all day,
Sipping some really tasty fruit cocktails.

She gets richer by the day,
From her and her husband's job.
All they have to do
Is lounge around all day.

She is very independent,
And can do things herself.
All her friends offer to help,
But she always tells them *no!*

Scott Eccleshall (10) John Bamford Primary School

SUNFLOWER

Show-off is the sunflower,
Though fun lover as well,
Very happy and friendly,
Lounging by the pool.

Doing her favourite hobby,
Going for a swim,
Getting dried and dressed again,
Putting on her party dress.

Going out mixing with friends,
Dressed up with makeup,
A cheerful 'Hello' to everybody,
Feeling really proud.

Adam Seager (9) John Bamford Primary School

ROSE

The rose can be a terrifying teacher,
Snapping at all the children,
She even frightens the parents.
With her thorny short temper!
But when she comes home from work,
She can be the most romantic person
you've ever seen.
Old and tall but very pretty is the rose,
The rose is harmful and very smart,
Rose is snooty when she walks
around the school,
The rose is our head mistress.

Robert O'Gorman (10) John Bamford Primary School

41

WATER

The waves crashing, splashing
Rumbling and foaming with fumes
Crashing against rocks
I can swim in it, I feel rain.
It makes puddles, water reflects.
Water gets you wet and it drips.
It can go in to bubbles and it makes mud.

Nicholas Russell (9) Landywood Primary School

ROARING LIKE A LION

Water roaring
Like a
Lion
The waves roaring
Water is hot
And is cold
As peaceful as church.
Water is wet
It can be salty
It can be calm.

Laura Edwards (9) Landywood Primary School

WATER IS GOOD

Water is wet, water is good for you.
Water crashes against the rocks.
Water splashes against the rocks.
Water, water still as a rock.
Water can be rain.
Water can be dripping rain.
Water is cold and hot.
Water can be ice.
Water is chlorine.
Water is wet, wet, wet and cold.

Gemma Allcock (9) Landywood Primary School

WATER

Water is good,
Water is cold,
Water is flowing everywhere.
Water is calm, soft and gentle and water is everywhere.
Water is salty.
Water is everywhere.
Water is refreshing,
Water is stagnant.
Water can be refreshing, calm and gentle.
Water is life.

Sam Card (9) Landywood Primary School

SAVE OUR WORLD

Save our world
Save our life
Work together
To end our strife.

Children are crying
Animals are dying
We as children
Must never give
up trying.

Kayleigh Cornes (10) Newstead Primary School

FAT CATS

Fat cats, fat cats they are *great!*
Fat cats they eat rats all day.
Fat cats like to play
That's why fat cats are so *great!*

Fat cats, fat cats they scare lots of people,
Fat cats, fat cats they smell so much,
Fat cats their little legs carry them so fast,
That's why fat cats are *great!*

Fat cats, fat cats they don't like dogs,
Fat cats, fat cats they sneak into your house,
So keep your windows shut and doors locked,
That's why fat cats are *great!*

Phillip Marsh (10) Newstead Primary School

HANDS

Hands are very useful in many different ways,
You can write with them you can type with them.
You can even tie a tie with them.

You can pick flowers and put them in a vase,
You can even eat a chocolate bar that's named Mars.

Without them you cannot pray,
Without them you cannot play,
So look after your hands and keep them clean,
And never use them to be mean.

Claire Walford (10) Newstead Primary School

HANDS

Hands you can use every day. Almost in every way.
You can play and pray. You can play on a computer,
and play with your toys, and play with your friends
the girls and boys.

You can cook and clean and do the washing
without a machine, and you can do the gardening too.

You can use your hands every day. Use them all the
years in every way. Hands can be handy for holding
chocolate candy, you can type with them and write
with them too.

Liam Johnson (10) Newstead Primary School

TREES

Trees! Trees! We couldn't live without them.
Trees! Trees! They are all around,
Trees! Trees! We breathe the oxygen
Trees! Trees! Give us our sound!

Trees! Trees! Such beautiful things.
Trees! Trees! They are living too,
Trees! Trees! So stop cutting them down.
Because you wouldn't like someone to cut down you!

If you cut down more trees
There will be no living things
So don't cut down trees
Or else we will all die.

Lesley Mountford (10) Newstead Primary School

BUTTERFLY

Once I saw a butterfly,
it was bright yellow and red.
It flew almost anywhere
but it did not fly near the lake
it was flying around in circles
for hours on end
but then it stopped and lay on a leaf
for the rest of the day.

Nicola Edwards (10) Newstead Primary School

THE FOREST OF TREES

I went for a walk one sunny day
I saw a willow tree on the way,
Next to the willow there stood a big oak
It made me think of a funny joke.

Then I went on and saw
The biggest and widest sycamore,
Right next to that there stood a small tree
It was the smallest I ever did see.

Then I saw ahead of me
Someone had cut down a long pine tree,
I felt so sad I nearly cried
That poor pine tree has now died.

Richard Whitehurst (10) Newstead Primary School

FRIENDS

I have lots of friends, at school
At least until the day ends
I like to play
In the day
With all of my friends.

I have Catherine and Debbie,
And Lesley and Kayleigh,
And I have a friend called Pat.
But best of all when I get home I have my cat!

Kayleigh Bird (9) Newstead Primary School

THE WIND

The wind it travels through my hair,
And travels with great care,

The wind it flows through the trees,
To make them rustle in the breeze,

The wind it goes around the world,
With such delight and strength,

The wind it knows where to go,
In the night and day.

Kimberley Dutton (11) Newstead Primary School

MY KITTEN

I have a kitten
Her name is Jessie.
She is black and white.
And we play ball together
First I flick a little ball
Then whack!
It goes against the wall.

Natasha Baddeley (10) Newstead Primary School

WIGGLY WORM

Wiggly worm wiggle through the soil.
Have a nice slither.
Roll and twist and
Sun-bathe in the wct grass.
And at night slither home.

Grace Hutchinson (7) Norton Canes Primary School

SOUNDS AND NOISES

Rain, thunder, lightning, snow,
Crash, bang, wallop, go.
Twist, turn, bang, bounce,
Hip, hop, ping, tang,
Whip, whop, wing, wang.
Whish, whosh, drip, plop.
Mish, mash, zig, zag,
Slig, slog, wig, wag,
Fire flames burning hot,
Bubbling stew in the pot.
Ice cold fridge-freezer,
Running water, what a teaser.
My rhyme is now over as you see,
Just two more sound words,
Hooray, whoopeeeeeeeeeeeeeeeee!

Kelly Cadman (11) Norton Canes Primary School

ONE SUMMER'S DAY

One summer's day the trees were making shadows -
And the leaves are bronze and green.
Branches are making arch ways over our heads -
And the trees are dressed in green.
The daisies are in bud and flower with white petals tipped with pink.
A butterfly alighted on a tree
Then fluttered lazily away
Branches on trees grab at people walking by.

Jenna Claye (10) Norton Canes Primary School

THE SNOW

My feet are cold but I don't care
As long as I see this snow.
It glistens it's cold but I don't care
The view is enough for me.
Deserted football pitch covered in snow
The sun beats on the snow
Soon it will be gone
So let's enjoy the snow while it's here
Let's not wait until next year.
The icicles hanging dripping and cold
Make my bones shiver in the cold
The treetops glisten shadows on
The snow
The soft wind blowing against my face.

James Whittaker (10) Norton Canes Primary School

ONE WINTER'S MORNING

One winter's morning,
Snow was softly there,
Plants buried in snow,
Nobody's there to say hello,
I'm freezing cold but I don't care,
All I can see is a cotton sheet, in front of me,
Snow calmly on the floor,
Have you seen it face to face,
Rows of footprints door to door,
Football pitch all alone,
No football there to see,
Skeleton trees bare with snow,
No birds to come and stay.

Rebecca Bate (9) Norton Canes Primary School

A SNOWY WINTER'S DAY

Soft snow brunching softly together,
Bushes buried in snow,
Sparkling cobwebs like tennis rackets,
What ever could happen next?

Footprints of small animals?
Sparkling snow like glitter and crystal ,
Picnic tables like marshmallow biscuits,
Snow is like soft and fluffy wool,
Icicles that glisten from roof tops,
Water frozen in drain pipes,
Fingers and feet go stone cold.

Carly Simpson (10) Norton Canes Primary School

THE MONSOON

Before the monsoon,
It's very hot.
And the days are endless and dry,
Sweltering people are very tired,
And the ground is hard and dusty.

The clouds opened
And the rain poured out,
And it rained -
            And rained -
                    And rained!
Umbrellas burst open,
And people sprang to life.

David McCracken (11) Norton Canes Primary School

RAINBOW COLOURED ICICLES

Silently the wind is blowing,
Here there and everywhere,
My feet and hands are very cold,
But why should I care at all.

Icicles icicles everywhere,
We are always seeing icicles
Shimmering of pink and blue,
That is what they really do.

Pink and blue that can't be right,
Are you sure that it is true?
Yes I am, I'm not lying.
Why should I there's no reason to.

Burning red sun in a brilliant blue sky
Is shining on the icicles,
Making them shimmer
With pink, blues and greens.

Emma Wallage (10) Norton Canes Primary School

WINTER MORNING

My hands are freezing but I don't mind.
Snow is here to slip and slide.
My feet are crunching in the snow.
Fireball sun shining.
Making long shadows on the snow.
Trees like skeletons rising up from the snow.
Powdery football pitch like marshmallow biscuits.
My feet are cold but I don't care.
At least I have some clothes to wear.

Lee Prince (10) Norton Canes Primary School

EURO 96

Euro 96 has now started,
And Gazza has not yet blarted,
So come on down to Wembley,
Where all the fans are trembly,
And Wembley is the home of the English team,
We beat Scotland, Wales and Ireland,
And were really mean
We thrashed Holland and the Scottish side,
But with Switzerland we lied,
England are going through,
And that is true,
We've beaten all the rest,
Because we're the best,
I don't know whether we're going to win the cup,
But one thing I know,
England's going up
Terry Venables, is leaving after Euro 96,
And Glenn Hoddle is coming in with some sneaky,
Tricks.

Mark Turu, James Ward, Adam Shaw (11) Norton Canes Primary School

GLISTENING SNOW

Winter wonderland glistening snow
That's where children like to go
Freezing feet but I don't care
I need wellingtons to play out there.
The bushes are buried in white snow
That's where children shouldn't go
Icicles are like crystals there.
They look like Jack Frost's fingers
And his hair.

Colin Davis (10) Norton Canes Primary School

MONSOON

Months of sweltering and endless sunny days
Airless, dusty, dry parched sunny days.
Sun beating on our faces.
Rays eating into the ground.
People losing energy . . .

The clouds burst open everywhere
Then it
>   Rains
>   And rains
>   And rains
Umbrellas burst open
People spring to life.

Claire Wilson (11) Norton Canes Primary School

MONDAY MORNING

It's Monday morning half past eight,
I've got to go to school or I'll be late,
I'd better go because I'm meeting Gemma at the gate,
I hate Monday mornings at half past eight!

I go into class and slam the door,
Then my friend Emma starts to bawl,
Then my teacher enters the room,
And said you better get out your work or you'll
Miss your breaktime,
It's chaos at this time of day,
So I will be glad when we go out to play.

Louise Pritchard (11) Norton Canes Primary School

ON WINTER MORNINGS

On winter mornings I wake up,
And find that everything is covered up,
Everything glistens like gems in flour,
I wonder what it is,
It's snow!
Fluffy white blankets of snow,
Icicles!
They look like Jack Frost's fingers,
Bushes are buried,
They are all white,
Tree skeletons in the field,
I can't wait to go outside,
Making tracks my feet get cold,
My feet hurt,
Everywhere's deserted, lonely, silent,
I'm shivering cold.

Kerry Seery (10) Norton Canes Primary School

SNOWY DAY

Snow is crunching under
My feet,
Day by day
Snow sparkling just like
Diamonds
Slippy and slidey I don't care
Icicles dripped everywhere

Anthony Healy (10) Norton Canes Primary School

SMOOTH BLANKET OF SNOW

Smooth blanket of snow,
I feel I can snuggle up inside.
Play hide and seek,
Under the snow the best place
To hide

Smooth blanket of snow,
Hurry up back in the house
Drink a cup of tea,
Put cheese out for the mouse.

Smooth blanket of snow,
Feet making a smooth sound
Always feet freezing,
Icicles twirly and round.

Elizabeth Crockford (10) Norton Canes Primary School

WINTER WONDERLAND

Fluffy cold snow has fallen has fallen,
All over the winter wonderland.
No-one has ever been here before, ever lasting snow,
No trails not even the slightest paw print, quiet and lonely.
Snow glistens as the sun shines,
Like glitter on a Christmas card,
The football pitch sparkles as snow lies still.
Icicles hang on gutter, like Jack Frost's fingers,
Dragon's breath is misty,
Pale blue sky stretches far and wide,
No clouds are seen.
Footprints can be followed,
With a silent crunch,
Quiet and lonely.

Alison Smith (10) Norton Canes Primary School

A SNOWY MORNING

Outside everything is covered with a deep blanket of snow.
A tingle of cold bites each toe.
The snow has fallen, it's here today,
Jack Frost has been out to play.
There are crystals all over the floor.
Mr Frost has been door to door.
An avalanche when you shake a bush!
The sudden whirlwind is in a rush!
Icicles all sizes, big and small.
The over-hanging snow looks like it's going to fall.
The winter birds sing along -
What a wonderful winter song.
Winter isn't that bad after all -
Except for the sudden winter fall.

Stuart Carter (10) Norton Canes Primary School

SNOWY MORNING

Outside everything is covered with a deep blanket of snow.
Whoever brings it, I'll never know.
Icicles hang from the roof,
Like a frozen waterfall.
The big ball of the sun is so very bright,
That makes the world a wonderful sight.
The birds are chirping all around,
As they make that wintry sound.
There is a muffled sound,
As I step on the snowy ground.

Richard Green (10) Norton Canes Primary School

SNOWY MORNING

I see the snow upon the roof,
Icicles hanging down,
The world seems unreal.
A picture postcard upon the snowy scene.

I see the snow glistening upon the garden pond.
I hear the birds singing - singing softly above me.
The distant sound of traffic
I can hear behind me.

The garden bench looks like a marshmallow good enough to eat.
The snow is glistening and sparkling like caster sugar on a cake.
I see the sun coming out - a big ball come to melt our fun.

Laura Evans (10) Norton Canes Primary School

SUMMER SILENCE

As I walk through a secret garden,
I hear the leaves rustling together.
The birds sing endless songs.
And distant traffic rushes by.
The trees wear green leafed coats.
And the grasses dance together.
Butterflies flutter by -
Landing on plants on the way.
In the grass the dandelions' heads wait to blow away in the breeze.
The sound of silence fills the air.

Joanna Wood (10) Norton Canes Primary School

SNOW AT SCHOOL

Snow is like cotton wool,
My feet are very cold,
Plants are buried in ice snow,
No-one has ever been here before,
Never before,
All I can see is a sheet of snow by me,
The snow is crunching on the floor,
Trees have branches like a skeleton's fingers,
The picnic benches look like marshmallow biscuits,
Sun shining on the snow,
Making a beautiful glimmer,
No players are on the football pitch,
Everywhere's deserted, lonely, silent,
No-one has ever been here before
Never before.

Victoria Jordan (10) Norton Canes Primary School

NATURE

Trees, trees, sleeping until spring -
Waking when summer comes.
Green leaves open on the trees.
Flowers explode with colour into summer.
Heat is beaming, beaming, hot!
Sun is gleaming on the trees.
Spider's webs decorate pipes and trees.
In the silence only the trees rustle,
Buds begin to grow.
In the green house weeds are growing up the walls
Wonderful butterflies float past with lovely colours on them.

Joanne Widdowson (10) Norton Canes Primary School

THE SNOW

Outside a blanket of snow
Lies on the ground.
A mini avalanche falls to
The ground.
It falls off a bush.
As we walk the icicles
Melt to nothing.
A cold breeze passes me as
I walk through the cold snow.
The snow crunches as I walk,
The white flowers of winter sparkle
As I pass.
My feet tingle in the wet snow.
The gentle chirp of birds
In the cold breeze -
A few colours in the distance -
A glimmer of red and
Three evergreens covered in
White snow.
Children shouting and throwing
Snow at each other
People have fun
Everybody has fun in the
Snow.

Robert Cope (10) Norton Canes Primary School

SUMMER DAYS

The bumble bees buzz past the trees
Collecting pollen. Daisies dazzle in the sun,
And buttercups shine a brilliant gold.
Birds are twittering in the green coated trees.
Spider webs are wrapped around the branches.
Roses sparkle in the sun
The blossom makes you sneeze.
And trees give a cool breeze.
In the long grass dandelion heads are
Waiting to float away with the breeze
The rhododendron claws around
The deserted green house.
The sun shines on the trees
And makes patterns on the benches.
We can hear distant traffic if we are quiet.

Emily Anne Murcott (10) Norton Canes Primary School

CHILLY POEM

F rost is a winter. Melting all the hotness
    Slam goes the door till next spring.

R oads are freezing at night but in the
    Morning they're sunny and bright.

O ther than pointed and sharp jagged at night
    It is always slidey in the light.

S unny and bright in the morning pointed and
    Sharp in the night

T ent hole and cracks for poor old Jack.

Stephen Mogan (8) St Chad's Primary School, Lichfield

A FROST POEM

F riday's a frosty day

R unning water down the icicles

O ther people nice and warm

S teaming kettles in the house and

T rampering feet on the ground.

William Hicks (9) St Chad's Primary School, Lichfield

A HAIKU POEM

Summer, autumn, winter and spring
Summer sun, autumn leaves and winter snow
What does the other bring

Cherrelle Coleman (9) St Chad's Primary School, Lichfield

FROST

*F*reezing frost on Friday
*R*ound your window pane
*O*ver the path and covering roads
*S*hining sun we wish you were here
*T*he seasons are turning again

James Edwards (9) St Chad's Primary School, Lichfield

THE SKY

The sky is blue,
The sky is red,
Shut up, I say,
Just go to bed.

> The sky is red,
> The sky is pink,
> *When your exams come,*
> *You have to think, think, think.*

The sky is green,
The sky is blue,
Get out, I say,
Just shoo, shoo, shoo!

Laura Ferguson (10) St Chad's Primary School, Lichfield

PIRATES

One windy day as we set sail we heard
Some pirates as we went through the gale
We were not sailing for long
As we heard the dong
And the pirates were eventually in sight.
We heard fire, fire and the ship went down
We were swimming for our life and we didn't want to drown
We split up and I swam to an island
And guess what I saw . . .
   Pirates!

Ruairi Edwards (8) St Chad's Primary School, Lichfield

BLUEBIRDS

Bluebirds flutter round my garden
On a summer's day . . .
Twitter twitter toodle-doo
Bluebird, how I do love you!

You are smart,
And you are blue.
Bluebird, how I do love you!

Joanne Talbot (8) St Chad's Primary School, Lichfield

A WINTER POEM

F ire in the cold homes
R oads are scattered in ice
O utside the window ledge
S cattered trees and frosty hedge
T ime goes by to summer and spring.

Liam Bradley (9) St Chad's Primary School, Lichfield

FROST, FREEZING FROST

F reezing frost, freezing fog
R unning down our window pane
O ut come the children all warm and snug
S tiff and crisp are the spider's webs
T he trees are glistening white

Thomas Mould (9) St Chad's Primary School, Lichfield

FROST

*F*rost comes on Friday morning
*R*ain drops coming down in an evening
*O*pen the door and look there's the snow
*S*pider's web covered with frost
*T*he frost is out again

Lizzie Sear (8) St Chad's Primary School, Lichfield

FROST

*F*rosty days in winter evenings
*R*ain drops on the spider's web
*O*n a Friday morning
*S*unny days we wish were here
*T*he frost is out clear and shining

Alana Smetham (9) St Chad's Primary School, Lichfield

FROST

F og in the morning, frost at night
R oads are icy, you snuggle up tight
O ut comes Jack Frost, in goes the sun
S o stay indoors and have some fun
T o get rid of the frost and bring out the sun

Tim Allen (8) St Chad's Primary School, Lichfield

THIS IS MY WEATHER POEM

Summer days are hot
Winter days are cold
The sun is like a ball of gas
The frost is like sparkling glass
Lightning strikes on the clouds
Thunder crashes to the ground
The rainbow glistens in the sky
Rain drips to the ground.

Hannah Prouse (9) St Chad's Primary School, Lichfield

A WINTER POEM

Frost in the morning
Round the window pane
Outside is cold
Spider's webs are frozen
The frost is out again

Elouisa Holton (9) St Chad's Primary School, Lichfield

FROST

F reezing frosty weather tonight
R ound and round Jack Frost goes sprinkling frost over the land
O ver the world he runs
S oon the sun will be back, hopefully
T here will be more frost next year probably

Alex Lee (8) St Chad's Primary School, Lichfield

FROST

*F*riday frost
*R*unning down the window pane
*O*ut comes the frost
*S*un goes in
*T*he frost is sparkling

Sarah Bax (8) St Chad's Primary School, Lichfield

THOUGHT FOR THE FUTURE

I am the fish
I live in the sea
People catch me
For their tea.

I am the pig
I live in a sty
People want pork
So I must die.

I am the cow
I live on the farm
People like beef
So they cause me harm.

Child says to its mother
What was a cow?
They won't know
If you eat us *now!*

Marie Morris (10) St Chad's Primary School, Lichfield

TIME

School time
Rule time
What a boring cruel time

Play time
Gay time
What a happy day time

Bed time
Sleepy head time
Favourite books are read time

Steven Morris (9) St Chad's Primary School, Lichfield

THE MAGIC SHOW

Magic this, magic that!
What comes out of the magic hat?
Rabbit ears and a pure white dove,
And a butterfly from above.

Sparks and twinkles from my wand . . .
Out pops a goldfish from the pond.
Abracadabra, zippy da-doo
Turn it into a kangaroo.

My show is over
All is done
Whiz, pop, bang!
And I am gone . . .

Paul Talbot (10) St Chad's Primary School, Lichfield

THE FIRE MONSTER

Deep in the boiling belly,
Of the volcano,
The fire monster sleeps,
Wisps of smoke from his nostrils,
Squeeze through cracks,
In the crater's mouth.

Deep in the boiling belly,
Of the volcano,
The fire monster roars,
Huge chunks of rock spit from his nostrils,
Red torrents of lava shoot through the sky,
Then stream down the crater's sides.

In the village in the valley,
The watchers wait,
For the fire monster's anger to abate.

John Radcliffe (11) St Chad's Primary School, Lichfield

AUTUMN

Leaves are falling in the autumn winds
Leaves are dancing in the autumn winds
Chestnuts are falling.
When the sun dies down.
And by night there is not a sound.
And by morning.
The hedgehogs are snoring.

Emma Tonks (8) St Dominic's Priory School, Stone

MY SWORD BY A VIKING

My sword you are the one
The only one I have,
You will be the one I have forever,
And when I go to heaven
You will be with me all the time,
When we go to fight
You will be with me,
I feel you in my hand,
And when I see you,
You glitter in the dark,
And in the morning.

Katherine Shanahan (8) St Dominic's Priory School, Stone

SPRINGTIME

Spring is in the air
Glistening in the sun
All the leaves are growing back
Now winter and autumn are done,
Baby lambs are skipping in the fresh green meadows
Early morning singing, the busy birds fly high
Flowers blooming
Daffodils golden, gleaming in the sun
Crocus of many colours fluttering in the cool air
Buttercups dancing in the summer breeze
Blossoms like fluffy white clouds delicate pinks and white
Tulips like toy soldiers red and yellow in the garden
Poppies in the meadows swaying in the sun
That's what I like about springtime when winter and autumn are done.

Fiona James (9) St Dominic's Priory School, Stone

MY TEDDY

Teddies come in shapes and sizes
But it's my teddy that wins all the prizes.
He's old and scruffy with a droopy eye
But smiles and loves me when I cry,
He guards my bed when I'm at school
He just sits there and waits for me
He's so cool.

His clothes are few and his tummy only grunts
But the love between us is what counts.
I love him dearly that's all I know
And I wouldn't change him for any so and so
        His name is Nuffy Jones!

Rosanna Jones (8) St Dominic's Priory School, Stone

SUMMER

Summer is my best season.
It makes me happy,
Like a bird singing a summer
Song.
I really like summer.
There is another reason,
Why I like summer. I shall
Tell you now.
I like it because I can get
My rabbit out
To play.

Ellie Davies (8) St Dominic's Priory School, Stone

MY DOG

I take my dog for walks
He loves it
He is golden like corn
He acts like a puppy
We tickle his tummy
Most important of all
He is the best dog in the world.

Lauren Tompkinson (8) St Dominic's Priory School, Stone

MY WENDY HOUSE IS NO MORE

Daddy built me a Wendy house with curtains white and blue
He put plastic for the windows so I could see out through.
It had a little chimney and a sloping, green felt roof
(My daddy put the felt up to make it waterproof).

I used to take my teddies in and give them cups of tea,
And all my little friends came round to play in there with me.
When I was cross I used to sit upon a chair inside
But mummy always knew it was the place where I would hide.

I played in it for several years, he made it when I was two
It's been a house, a school, a shop, it's even been a zoo!
But now I'm nine I've grown quite old, I don't need it anymore
So since last Sunday afternoon, my Wendy is no more!

It had got in a state, my Wendy, ivy had grown through the floor
The plastic had gone from the windows and I couldn't open the door.
So daddy went out with a hammer and started to take it apart
I couldn't bare to watch him it almost broke my heart.

Now there is space in the garden where the Wendy used to be
It's a dark and gloomy corner under the cherry tree.
I'd like a new swing, or a slide, or maybe my own flower bed
But I know my dad, he plans to put up a shed!

Rebecca Thomas (9) St Dominic's Priory School, Stone

HEDGEHOGS

Hedgehogs roam and crawl around,
Making a kind of snuffling sound.
If the hedgehog has a fright,
In the day or in the night,
He rolls himself into a tiny ball,
So nothing can really harm him at all.
He eats insects and sometimes mice
A diet which he finds extremely nice!

Helena Somervail (8) St Dominic's Priory School, Stone

LITTLE MONSTERS

My sister is two
She has got blue eyes and curls that are gold
My mum says she is an angel
But she *never* does as she is told.
She gobbles down beetles and devours worms
I mean,
How could you eat something
That squiggles and squirms
My sister is so greedy and
Her manners are gross
She tips up her dishes and
Rips up her toast.
My relations think
That she will be a politician one day
I object strongly, but they just say,
Oh,
She's so good, so delightful,
So pink and so fat.
But I don't think she's
Anything like that.

Ffion Carlin (9) St Dominic's Priory School, Stone

LONDON

London is big,
London is famous,
London is the home of our Queen,
Who knows?
She could be seen

London at night,
Is busy and bright,
Millions of people,
Rushing here and there,
People in clothes,
That I would not wear
All different people,
From all round the world,
Come to visit London, to see
What they can see.

Davina Charlton (8) St Dominic's Priory School, Stone

MY DOG

My dog is playful
He is very clever too
Life is never ever dull
When he has something to chew

He sometimes makes a squeaky noise
When he is feeling sad
So I go and get his toys
Then he doesn't feel so bad.

Philip Edwards (8) St Dominic's Priory School, Stone

AUTUMN

I see the conkers falling,
And the reddening berries on the bushes,
I hear the rustling
And the crunching
Beneath my feet.

I feel the air getting colder.
I see the leaves
Changing colour in autumn.

Kimberley Addison (8) St Dominic's Priory School, Stone

FOOTBALL

On my birthday
I had a treat,
It was a goal post
From Uncle Pete,
It was the best thing I had
It was set up by my Dad.

A football game
Is so much fun.
I love to play
Out in the sun.
I kick the ball
So very high,
And as it lands
I race on by.

Andrew Flather (8) St Dominic's Priory School, Stone

MY CAT

My cat loves trees,
She climbs them,
The one by the washing line,
She likes the best.
She sharpens her claws,
She sits on the highest branch,
Her coat is shining black,
Her green eyes
Sparkle in the sun,
Grow bigger in the dark,
She likes it lots,
When I stroke her,
At bed time she curls herself up,
At the end of my bed.

Rebecca Ford (8) St Dominic's Priory School, Stone

MY SPECIAL DADDY

My daddy is a special man
He's very nice and kind
He mows the lawn and cleans the cars
Where does he find the time?
I think he is very cute
His tummy is so cuddly
I cannot find the words to say
I love him more every day

Kelly Holland (8) St Dominic's Priory School, Stone

PARROTS

Parrots are bright,
They sleep in the night
They wake in the morning
A new day yawning,
They eat nuts at meal times
And sometimes they nibble
At the big juicy limes
They fly high in the sky
They hide in the trees
They look like leaves

Rhiannon Caudwell (8) St Dominic's Priory School, Stone

MY TWO DOGS

One is big and one is small.
One is short and one is tall.
One likes brandy one likes gin.
One's called Jack and one's call Jim.

One is brown and one is black.
One is thin one is fat.
One chews shoes one digs holes.
One chases mice one chases moles.

Even though these dogs are different
I love them both in every way.

Jodi Bradbury (9) St Dominic's Priory School, Stone

SAMMY THE DOG

My dog Sam is a cheerful little chappie,
He runs like the wind and is always
Very happy.
He is always pleased to see us, when
We come home at night.
His ears are very dangley and his tail very waggy.
He likes to play in the hay and doesn't get in the way.
He jumps in the river and likes eating liver.

Katie Adamson (9) St Dominic's Priory School, Stone

THE SNAKE

Snakes are creatures
With many many features,
They move in a slither
Without a dither.

They coil in a spring
And can do anything,
They like lots of food
So don't catch them in a mood.

They live in the leaves
In the roots of the trees,
Their camouflage is good
Because they look like wood.

In the autumn they sleep
And don't make a peep,
When the spring comes
They bring little ones.

Zoe Maiden (9) St Dominic's Priory School, Stone

ROTTEN RESTAURANT

I went to a restaurant one day
they said it was beautifully laid
I tried a bit of this, a bit of that
Oh
What a taste it made
potatoes like Blu-Tac
sausages like rock
I couldn't even bite into the baked beans
Oh what a shock!

Dessert
ice-cream, chocolate and biscuits
I'm going to risk it
Ice-cream like gravel
chocolate like mud
biscuits like sawdust
Now I know how they got their name!

Gemma Brunt (9) St Dominic's Priory School, Stone

WHAT YOU CAN DO WITH A COMPUTER

You can:
C   Copy from me
O   On my big black screen
M   Maybe even play on me
P   Put disks in my pocket
U   Use them for games
T   Take disks out and change them again
E   Even use me for accounts
R   Right, left or up and down the keys will show
                                       you around or
S   Surf the Internet.

Charlie Cooper (10) St Dominic's Priory School, Stone

MY PET DRAGON

My pet dragon has four legs
He sits in the laundry and plays with the pegs
He has big green eyes and eats lots of flies
And if we don't feed him he cries and cries
He sleeps in the shed and makes his own bed
He frightens the neighbours out of their wits
He always breaks my Lego models into bits
But there's one thing I like about my pet dragon Dale
Is the fun that I have when I ride on his tail.

Georgina Frieder (9) St Dominic's Priory School, Stone

MY CAT

My cat has a black
and white head.
During the morning
he sleeps on my bed
He has four feet,
but he's missing a toe.
And follows me wherever I go
His tail is black with
a white kink.
When I go to bed he
gives me a wink.

Harriet Bell (9) St Dominic's Priory School, Stone

MY PUPPY

A round ball of fluff with teddy bear feet,
and a black stubby nose.

A barking machine that won't switch off
except when he's asleep.

One extra at the table staring longingly at my
plate hoping for titbits.

A small whirlwind biting at the breeze
while chasing leaves.

A bundle of dust from digging up the
garden looking for trouble.

A wagging tail when I come home from
school.

And a sloppy licking welcome from my
puppy *Boris.*

Sarah Passmore (9) St Dominic's Priory School, Stone

MY COMPUTER

I switch on the power then I can explore,
   My desktop keyboard and the monitor;
      In my computer I have an Internet,
         Where I can chat with people I haven't met,
            CD ROM, floppy disks sound like quite a fright,
               But just you wait until you get to the megabytes.
               CDs on the screen take me from the house
               And all just because I'm playing with
                                    the mouse!

Samantha Jones (11) St Dominic's Priory School, Stone

MY FARM

My name is Rebecca
Becky for short
I go to St Dominic's School
Where I've always been taught

My home is Little Sugnall,
We look over Ecc-le-shall,
My daddy is a farmer
And he works in overalls.

We have a herd of milking cows,
We also grow some corn,
Daddy always seems so busy,
Mummy has to mow the lawns.

Softy is my little pony
We really have great fun.
She sometimes tries to tip me off
But I manage to stay on.

Matthew is my little brother
He has a favourite cat,
A collie dog, two Schnauzer pups,
A bike, a ball, a bat.

It really is a lovely place
To grow up on a farm
As long as you don't mind the smells
Or come to any harm.

Rebecca Holmes (9) St Dominic's Priory School, Stone

COMPUTER BEEP

Beep beep beep,
Goes the keyboard in front
of the seat.
I am trying to get into a
file but it keeps on making a
Beep! Beep! Beep!
I hate this noise
it never gives me joys
so I just decided to go and play with my
toys. *Beep! Beep! Beep!*

Amy Baker (11) St Dominic's Priory School, Stone

THE COMPUTER

It sits there on my desktop
A sad and lonely computer
Then I came into the room
I turn it on and the light came up
Like a beam from the screen.

I worked all day
Finding information I would say
Making documents and files
Finding out about the Nile.

Now my computer is happy in every way
because I use it every day.

Amy Sanders (11) St Dominic's Priory School, Stone

THE OAK TREE

The oak tree standing in our garden
Was planted not a hundred years ago
With its broad dark trunk
Its silvery leaves
And its snake like bows
Daffodils drift beneath it.
A seat is placed beside it
So people can sit and watch
The meadows swaying in the wind
I hope it never changes.

Teresa Fitzherbert (9) St Dominic's Priory School, Stone

MY OLD CAR

My old car is so rusty and dusty
But I love it very much
It makes such a noise
When I press the clutch

It squeaks and it leaks
When I'm travelling along
With its dings and its dongs
It sounds like a song

I love my old car
It's precious to me
I hope that I *never*
Lose the key

Sophie Ryan (9) St Dominic's Priory School, Stone

THE LITTLE LAMB

The little lamb is as light as a feather
I feel sorry when he is out in horrible
weather.
The little lamb is as soft as a
teddy bear
He has such a sweet little mer-er-er-er
The little lamb is fluffy and white
If I could catch him I would
hug him with all my might
This little lamb is the sweetest lamb
in the world.

Tamsin Sawyer (9) St Dominic's Priory School, Stone

FIRST SIGNS OF SPRING

First signs of spring I see,
Are butterflies dancing among the flowers.
When I come up the drive from school,
What do I see?
Daffodils, bluebells, snowdrops and
Blossom on the trees.

First signs of spring I see,
Are the little lambs and chicks
Coming into the world.
When we go for walks I see
Carpets of flowers all golden in colour,
Sparkling in the sun.

Katie Gough (9) St Dominic's Priory School, Stone

COMPUTERS

A computer for a present,
Wow gee whiz,
I'm glad it's mine rather that his,
Buttons here a mouse there,
It's getting frustrating I'm pulling my hair,
floppy disc or CD ROM,
Where's all this information coming from?
No need for books as a guide,
Trying to understand and learn,
Sharing with my sister, taking it in turns,
time rushes by as we push the keys,
It will help me with my homework ,
Teacher will be pleased.

Alexandra Evans (10) St Dominic's Priory School, Stone

THE INTERNET
(To be sung to the tune of Surfin' USA)

Surfin' through the Internet
what a wonderful day,
using Windows 95 to type a letter to my friend.
Using the mouse,
Using the keys,
using the monitor to see what we need.
We pick and choose what we like to do,
what a variety.
The mouse has gone crazy playing Solitaire,
in Mine Sweeper the mines are blasting everywhere.
I could surf the Internet all day doing my work and
play.

The Internet!

Abigail Frankish (11) St Dominic's Priory School, Stone

BROKEN DOWN

Microchips flying,
People fitting and dying,
Printers printing gibberish,
Engineers frowning a bit.

The net's gone nutty,
The web's gone wonky,
'Oh help.' People cry.

My Amstrad, my Wang,
Workaholics do yell,
Kilobytes clonking,
People jumping and crying.

Managers having kittens,
People putting on mittens,
For fears that their fingers will burn,
Beyond technology's repair.

Then everything stops,
Cleaners get out mops,
There is hardly any light,
'cause the office is closed
For the night.

Lydia Austen (11) St Dominic's Priory School, Stone

LAYLA

My dog is called Layla,
She likes to drive a trailer!
She used to be a sailor!
She sailed the seven seas!
She doesn't like beef and she doesn't like peas
When men dogs see her they fall to their knees!

Charlotte Heywood (9) St Dominic's Priory School, Stone

THE SEASONS' CYCLE

Winter
Wearing sweaters in two layers
Throwing snowballs with two players
The snow is deep and thick
It's cold now mum close the door quick!

Spring
The buds are now on the trees
The wasps are humming so are the bees
The flowers are budding, shooting up
I'll go for a walk and take my pup!

Summer
Hazy sun, warm and bright
Waiting forever for the night
Nice long walks with my friends
I hope this summer never ends!

Autumn
The leaves fall off the trees
And flutter off into the breeze
Like nature's litter
The time flies by, here comes winter.

Elizabeth Evans (9) St Dominic's Priory School, Stone

SOCCER

Shooting, tackling, hitting the ball,
And you hear the crowd roar.

Shooting, tackling, hitting the ball,
Celebrating when you score a goal.

Shooting, tackling, hitting the ball,
people sliding and getting fouled.

Shooting, tackling, hitting the ball,
the half-time whistle blown aloud.

We're on the ball once again,
Shooting, tackling with the pain.

Shooting, tackling, hitting the ball
and then you score another
      Goal.

Len Wright (10) St Elizabeth RC Primary School

SHOCK WAVE

Shock wave
Waiting and waiting to get on the ride

Shock wave
Feeling excited as you get on

Shock wave
Waving to the camera as you go down the small flume

Shock wave
Going up and up through the tunnel up to the big drop

Shock wave
Feeling so excited and thinking you want to get off
      Help! As you go around the bend.

Shock wave
Whoosh! Going down the big slope not knowing what's happening

Shock wave
It's ended can I go again?

Rachel Brownsword (11) St Elizabeth RC Primary School

TAMWORTH CASTLE

The entering of the doors
the chilling feeling down my spine.
Every step I take there's a creak,
The big dull towers looming over me.
Fighting in the mist of ye old Tamworth.

Thinking of battle,
All the men charging at the doors and wall.
Thinking of kings and banquets,
Fighting in the mist of ye old Tamworth.

Imagining that I was a brave knight,
Swinging my sword and holding up my shield
to clubs and swords.
Imagining the musket fire filling the doors with holes.
Fighting in the mist of ye old Tamworth.

Feeling the cold, chilling mist,
The spooky feeling of the haunted bedroom,
the cold steps leading to the Norman tower,
Fighting in the mist of ye old Tamworth.

Leaving the doors, the tower and the haunted bedroom,
Saying goodbye to the ghostly musketeers.
Fighting in the mist of ye old Tamworth.

Mark Roberts (10) St Elizabeth RC Primary School

THE OLD BARN

There is an old barn that I know,
It stands out there all alone.
The wind whistles,
And the trees blow,
But the barn I know,
Just stands out there all alone.

When I go in it comforts me,
It makes me feel at home.
There's hay on the floor,
And there's cracks in the door,
But I don't care,
This is my barn and I am safe here.

Ruth Baldwin (11) St Elizabeth RC Primary School

DO YOU KNOW WHAT THEY DID TO MY SON?

Crucify him! Crucify him!
The crowds went on.
Do you know what they did to my son?

Laughing at him
pulling his beard.
Do you know what they did to my son?

'Forgive them.' He said.
Astonished I was.
Do you know what they did to my son?

Crying out loud in pain
darkness appeared on the sixth hour.
Do you know what they did to my son?

Looking up at God, one last breath,
Do you know what they did to my son?

Gone now, dead, but there is hope.
Do you know what they did to my son?

He rose again that Easter morning.
The lord looked upon me.
My son has risen.

Lauren Holden (10) St Elizabeth RC Primary School

YE OLD TAMWORTH CASTLE

As you enter through the great oak doors
I step forward and the floor boards creak.
Ye old Tamworth Castle.

The towers loom over me,
The darkness makes me shiver.
Ye old Tamworth Castle.

I step into the haunted bedroom,
I feel the chill of the ghosts around me
Ye old Tamworth Castle.

Up the spiral staircase,
Going round and round getting dizzy, dizzy.
Ye old Tamworth Castle.

Think of the battles once fought here,
The flashing swords,
The shining armour
Ye old Tamworth castle.

I now leave the castle,
The winding stairs,
The old stone wall,
The old memories,
Ye old Tammworth Castle.

Matthew Henson (10) St Elizabeth RC Primary School

EASTER

One day I saw poor Jesus
Struggling up that hill.
With wood so hard and heavy
When he reached Calvary hill.
He was stripped of all his clothes.
And there was nailed to the cross
To die a terrible death.
The people cried and wept for him
While others just mocked and laughed
He died and gave us all new life.

Charlene Baker (11) St Elizabeth RC Primary School

CAMPING

It's raining,
The rain pattering on the tent,
like people tapping to get in.

The wind whistles,
like ghosts wailing.

Leaves rustling,
like teeth mashing.

The fire goes down,
like someone's red hot eyes
glowing outside.

Daniel Clark (10) St Elizabeth RC Primary School

WHAT DID HE DO?

They took him from the garden,
the garden of olives.
They took him up to Pilot,
the man whom all feared.
They all began to shout,
'Crucify him! Crucify him!'
The land was filled with shadows
But what did he do?

He drudged through the village,
praying as he went.
He trembled past his mother,
and fell at her feet.
His mother wept so bitterly,
as her dear boy stumbled by.
The land was filled with shadows
But what did he do?

They stripped his clothes so harshly,
and his eyes filled with tears.
They nailed him to the cross,
as if they didn't care.
The land was filled with shadows
But what did he do?

He died in pain and sorrow
He gave a mighty cry
To the Lord God our Saviour
And then he did die
He rose again on Sunday
and then we rejoice
For Jesus Christ our Saviour
As the land was filled with joy.

Dannielle Appleby (11) St Elizabeth RC Primary School

TAMWORTH CASTLE

Walking down the long black path,
Big, bare bushes looming over me.
The shadows looking like ghostly figures,
It sends a shiver down my spine.

Walking, in the grey. Old doorway,
Looking round at the broken, stone walls,
Stepping on the old floorboards,
that give a mighty creak.

Walking, into the great courtyard,
Thinking of so many knights fighting on this
floor,
Firing arrows at the door.

Walking, up the long, twisting steps,
Into the great big Norman tower.
Shields hanging on the walls.

Walking, onto the towering battlements,
Where so many knights once stood,
Looking down at the town beneath me,
Seeing far, far away in the distance.

Walking, into the haunted bedroom
A spooky shiver slides down my spine.
Hearing sighs and groans,
Seeing the black lady.

Walking, out of the castle,
Walking down the long, black path,
Big, bare bushes looming over me,
The shadows looking like ghostly figures.

Alex Henson (10) St Elizabeth RC Primary School

FORMULA ONE

Fast furious cars,
Flying through the air like a hot knife through
butter.
Noisy big monsters, lining up in rows,
The lights go out and off they go.
Hill, Coulthard, followed by Schumacher,
He is being chased by Berger and Alesi,

Racing, racing, racing.

Matthew Atkins (10) St Elizabeth RC Primary School

NO-ONE CARED

He travelled in pain on the road to Calvary hill,
He was nailed to the cross which had been
carried by the son of God himself.
No one cared,
they just stared.
He was taken down from the *Crucifix* and
placed in Mary's arms,
People protested but were held back by soldiers.
No-one cared,
They just stared.
He was buried in the cold damp tomb,
People grieved for days for no-one knew he would
die so young.
No-one cared,
They just stared.
He rose from the dead and saved us all,
Everyone cared.

Amy Cole (10) St Elizabeth RC Primary School

PYTHON

Climbing up the never ending slope,
Wondering oh wondering what would happen next.

Seemed like it would go on forever,
But at last the moment came.

Deafening screams were all I heard,
A blinding dip lay down below.

I closed my eyes and held on tight,
I was scared of that terrifying height.

I said to my brother 'When is this going to end?'
But the worst was just around the bend.

Down the dip, and up again
My thoughts and mind were full of fright.

I thought in my mind this is fun,
But then the loop the loop had not begun.

Down again the loop the loop,
And then came up with another scoop.

Slowed to a halt and gave a jolt,
I jumped out as quickly as a lightning bolt.

My dad was drinking from a tea cup,
That ride was definitely a thumbs up.

John Connor (10) St Elizabeth RC Primary School

TOWER OF TERROR

When you get on,
You wonder, what's going to happen?

When you're going up
You wonder, what's going to happen?

When you're half way,
You wonder, what's going to happen?

When you feel your tummy rumbling,
You wonder, what's going to happen?

When you get to the top,
You wonder, what's going to happen?

When it drops you a little way down,
You wonder, what's going to happen?

When it stops you half way,
You wonder, what's going to happen?

When it starts going back up,
You wonder, what's going to happen?

When it drops you down again,
You wonder, what's going to happen?

When you feel it hit the floor,
You wonder, what's going to happen?

When you feel your heart pounding,
You wonder, what's going to happen?

When you get off,
You think yeah that's great.

Jamie Sidaway (10) St Elizabeth RC Primary School

EASTER

'One of you is going
To betray me tonight.
Will you not go
To do your work?'

'And before the cock crows tonight
You will betray me three times
Simon Peter of Galilee.'

'Can you not stay awake?
Will you not watch
One hour with me?'

Now the Lord shall take the cross
And bear the weight upon him.
To reach the place where he shall die.

He is nailed to the cross
And the cross is in the ground
And the Lord is in great pain.

Now the Lord has died
And the temple is torn in two
And there's darkness over the land.

Jesus is placed
In his mother's arms
And John stands beside.

Jesus is buried
In a big tomb
But three days later
He has risen again!

Ruth Jordan (10) St Elizabeth RC Primary School

EASTER POEM

Easter means a lot to me,
Our King, Jesus died on the cross for us,
He rose again to save us.

Easter means a lot to me,
It means kindness and love,
Joy, happiness and sharing.

Easter means a lot to me,
It told me about, what happened to Jesus,
Now Jesus has risen it is time to celebrate.

Ben Wilkins (11) St Elizabeth RC Primary School

THE LUCKY SHOT

The desert, rainforest and the
brothers
Which are the poles,
Tossed the three sided coin and the
desert won.
The desert became gold with sand and
hot
So it was royal.

The rainforest was second.
It became hot and wet
So it became rich.

The brothers came last
And they were cold and wet
So they were lonely and forgotten.

It was only a piece of luck.

Thomas Halsted (8) St John's CE Primary School

THE WATER RACE

On the start line, brooks and streams gleam
With excitement,
Calm, waiting their turn.
Then off! Running down
Their track.

Then they grow muscular, swell into lakes,
Emerge as athletes-storming river -
And their time they *don't* take.
As they reach the end of the track,
They catapult over the precipice,
Hurtling waterfall.

Now the race is done,
As they throw themselves over
The finish line -
Collapsed!

Rebecca Davies-Thomas (11) St John's CE Primary School

QUIET NIGHTS

Quiet nights hearing the blink of
an eye;
people breathing soundlessly,
giving a sigh.

The footsteps of a stray dog,
the whistling of the wind,
the presence of the fog.

Blink blink goes a street light -
that's my idea of the dark quiet
nights.

David Travis (10) St John's CE Primary School

THE CAT

I had a cat once
but it was a pain:
it made a mess on the floor
and it scratched at the front door.
Mum went mad in the end,
and she said it had to go.

So then I got a dog
but it growled and barked in the night;
it gave my mum a big fright
and she said it had to go.

So I got a hamster,
but it nipped my mum
and it bit my dad's bum
and my dad said it had to go.

But then I got a sister;
she cried all night.
But - she had to stay!

Bradley Tooley (10) St John's CE Primary School

STORMS

The thunder, the rain it is such a pain.
It always ruins your day.
The thunder and lightning is so frightening
In a little tiny way.
When it starts to flash and to rumble,
We always grumble and grumble.
'Cos we can't go out to play.

Marc Malloy (11) St Mary's RC Primary School, Cannock

BADMINTON

As the shuttle-cock flies through the air,
I hit it with my racket then and there.
I swing my racket hard and good,
It travels twenty-four miles and goes up forty-two foot.
The game has ended, I'm very sad,
I lost to my partner so I'm also mad!
My partner's happy, but what would you expect,
She won the tournament,
She has become the best.
She receives the cup off the judge,
But she won fair and square, I don't hold a grudge.

Rebecca Langley (11) St Mary's RC Primary School, Cannock

999

I was sneezing and coughing and sick,
I went to the doctor so quick,
the doctor said 'Call 999! You can't go home in this state
I know these signs.'
An ambulance came, blue lights flashing,
And a noise that sounded like foxes dashing.
At the hospital, big doors swung open with a swish,
I went to a room with a lot of sick people who were asleep
of course.
I went to sleep in a bed that wasn't mine.
I woke in the morning and there were cornflakes in front of me,
hmm, very tasty.
The orange was nice the toast even better
Butter that melted on top
I went home with a smile on my face
I said goodbye.
Thanks a lot!

Thomas Muller (10) St Mary's RC Primary School, Cannock

MY SILVER STEED

Galloping over fields of wheat,
My silver steed has no defeat,
There is nothing more
That I adore,
Than the wind in my hair
On my beautiful mare.
the country going past,
Oh so, so fast.
We got back to the stable
mighty quick,
Within just a tails flick.
She has some water and
some bran.
I groom her down,
On my face no frown.
I sort out her tack,
Pull myself on her back.
Off we go again,
On back over the endless plain.

Sarah Davison (11) St Mary's RC Primary School, Cannock

THE TONGUE TWISTER

Pretty Polly picked Pickles parrot
From the parrot pet shop.
Pretty Polly took Pickles parrot
From the parrot pet shop.
Home to practise patter.
'Pretty Polly. Pretty Polly.' pattered Prickles
'Pretty Polly. Pretty Polly.' Pickles parrot pattered.

Carly Wall (10) St Mary's RC Primary School, Cannock

PIGS

Pigs, pigs
Mucky pigs
Rolling in mud as they play
If they could, they'd do this all day.

Pigs, pigs
Lazy pigs
In the sun as they bake
End up looking like a big pink cake.

Pigs, pigs
Greedy pigs
Guzzling their food in one go
It's no good trying to make them eat slow.

Pigs, pigs
Loveable pigs
Warm, friendly playful and funny
I wouldn't swap my pigs for any amount of money.

Samantha Jackson (11) St Mary's RC Primary School, Cannock

LUNCH TIME

I like lunch time because I get to eat!
The food I eat is mostly meat.
The meat I eat is Billy bear,
I eat it with sauce or eat it rare.
I always dream about lunch time,
Because I sometimes have a green juicy lime.
On occasions I have a lemon,
When I eat it I think I'm in heaven.

Stuart France (11) St Mary's RC Primary School, Cannock

ENVIRONMENT

Black haze over the sky
Whirling traffic below.
Smoke belching from chimney pots,
Litter blowing,
Traffic slowing,
Destruction to the Earth.
Forests falling,
Tractors trudging,
Oil slicks spreading, acid rain
Falling.
Elephants killed for their tusks,
Tigers for their skins.
Destruction to the earth
Destruction to the earth
Destruction to the earth.

Daniel Taylor (11) St Mary's RC Primary School, Cannock

WE SAT ON ...

We sat on the white cliffs of Dover,
While eating my mother's Pavlova.
I said, 'What a wonderful view,'
While the others argued about the first man who flew.
I just sat there admiring the sea,
I thought to myself, 'What's the matter,
This isn't like me?'
I had to prise myself away
At the end of a beautiful day,
There were almost tears in my eyes,
Sadness, I couldn't disguise.

Sara Reynolds (11) St Mary's RC Primary School, Cannock

THE WORD PARTY

Soft words pretend to be hard.
Naughty words rip up every Christmas card.
Kind words share their sweeties.
Smelly words have smelly feeties.
Heavy words make holes in the ground.
Quiet words do not make a sound.
Forgetful words forget where they are.
Fast words drive a racing car.
Slow words go very slow.
Hiding words come and go.

I have come
Now I must go.

Harriet Beeston (10) St Mary's RC Primary School, Cannock

I WISH

I wish I was an all time
Goalkeeper
And be like David Seaman
Or
Ian Walker
I wish I was a cricketer like
Mike Atherton,
Up into the crowd for six.
I wish I could be
A basketball player
And play for Chicago Bulls.

Thomas Lyonette (8) St Mary's RC Primary School, Cannock

HEDGEHOGS

Hedgehogs can eat most wonderful things,
From tiny beetles to giant hens' wings.
Hedgehogs walk around on tiny feet
Shuffling along through the wheat.
They roll up into a little ball,
In case the badgers eat them all.
Then for the winter they go to bed,
But wake up in the spring as
everyone said.

Katie Smythies (11) St Mary's RC Primary School, Cannock

EXCITEMENT!

Off goes a firework with a thrilling scream,
Looks as if it is a dream.
As sparks gently float, down, down, down.
Green and crimson or gold as a crown.

Whooshing, gushing a race to the sky,
Letting off flames as it does fly.
Suddenly a jump with fright,
As a beautiful display of light.
Clears the sky of black and gloom,
Pets shiver in an inside room.

Wrap up warm to enjoy the fun,
Yellow lights up the sky, as does the sun.
The smell of gunpowder in the air,
The moon finds it very unfair.
The crimson gold to end the night,
The time has come to say - 'goodnight.'

Sarah Carter (11) St Michael's School, Lichfield

WAR

As men walk.
To meet their doom.
Generals talk,
Not knowing how it feels.

As men go to sleep
In the trenches, so cold.
Generals sleep
In beds, so warm.

As men fight,
With bombs flying.
Generals light
The lamps in their rooms.

Bloody atmosphere of death
For the soldiers.
Generals sit cosily
In their dining rooms.

'Let us go to meet our doom,'
The soldiers say.
'As we get on the train
For Germany.'

Generals sit,
Watching them go.
They are laughing 'ha, ha,'
As they don't know.

Do not join the army.
Try to stop war.
For if it goes on,
You may fall!

Stephen Darby (11) St Michael's School, Lichfield

IT'S A SOLDIER'S LIFE

I'm scared, I'm petrified, I'm shaking with fear,
That battlefield tomorrow, I don't want to be near,
But now I'll rest and have some sleep,
For tomorrow's battle, dead men in a heap.

The sun is shining, the weather is mild,
Thinking of dying is driving me wild,
But now I'm ready to go out and fight,
To hope that after, I'll still have my life.

Bang, crash, boom, I don't want to be here,
Bombs exploding, I'm trembling with fear,
Oh no! My friends are getting shot down,
Blood spurting out, as they fall to the ground.

But the opposition are falling and dying as well,
Retreat! Retreat! Their captain does yell,
The trumpet blows, we've won the fight!
And I myself, still have my life.

James Brindle (11) St Michael's School, Lichfield

AFRICAN WILD CAT

This is a wild cat
Teeth like a vampire bat,
Claws as sharp as a big dagger
Enough to make a little mouse stagger
His markings make him look like a tiger
But luckily he's wrong size and colour.
He hisses and spits when angry or afraid
His fur is brown, black and cream
He is not as fierce as he may seem
Or is he?

Liam Clamp (11) St Modwens RC Primary School, Burton-On-Trent

THE FAT CAT

The fat cat always ate
With never a fear in mind
The fat cat always ate
His teeth always grind
The fat cat always ate
But he is very kind

The fat cat always ate
With a mysterious face
The fat cat always ate
Always in a race
The fat cat always ate
In a fast pace.

Nicola Williams (10) St Modwens RC Primary School, Burton-On-Trent

THE HUNGRY LION

Hot and tired the lion crawled back,
He was very sleepy, he needed a nap.
He rested his big hairy head gently on the ground,
And closed his mouth were his teeth would be found.
When he woke up he was in a hungry mood.
For some very, very, very tasty food.
His teeth were like daggers ready for action
To slice into his prey that would give him
Satisfaction.
He sees a zebra munching on some grass
He pounces onto it in one big flash.
He tears it open with his mountain peeked
Teeth and scoffs it all what a big feast.

Sarah Ann Shilton (11) St Modwens RC Primary School,
Burton-On-Trent

SPACE POODLES FROM MARS

Space poodles are crazy
Space poodles are mad
Space poodles are dangerous
Space poodles are bad

Space poodles can't fly
Space poodles can kill a nun
Space poodles are strong
Whatever you do don't give them a gun

Space poodles came from Mars
Space poodles can sail
If they just see two chocolate bars
They can never fail

Space poodles are big
Space poodles have a big bite
Space poodles are fat
They love to have a fight

Gavin Stamp (10) St Modwens RC Primary School, Burton-On-Trent

THE WOLF

The wolf has fur as white as snow and in the night
It shows.
And when the wind blows
The wolf will pose his long wild fur

The wolf has eyes as black as the sky
He could spot any bird and it will die

Adam Smith (11) St Modwens RC Primary School, Burton-On-Trent

THE MIDNIGHT WOOD

Dark in the midnight wood
What can I see?
I can see the moonlight shining over me
The bees are buzzing around the trees
Shadows creep around the leaves

Dark in the midnight wood
What could it be?
Could be a lake going
Through it, I swam
It could be a man
If it was, I run,
Run for my life.

Dark in the midnight wood
What can I fear?
Fear someone here I come so
Near finding bones over here,
'Here,' said someone 'hear what I say,'
I think you're very clever
But you'll be here forever!

Matthew Winson (11) St Modwens RC Primary School, Burton-On-Trent

GALAPAGOS HAWK

The hawk has a sharp pointed beak
His eyes sparkle in the sun.
He glides through the sky.
      He stops.
He hovers and swoops
Down he sticks his claws into
The rat
And carries it back to his young.

James Bell (11) St Modwens RC Primary School, Burton-On-Trent

THE OWL

Every dark night the owl flies
His big wings spread out wide
He swoops and glides and stunts he tries
The owl, in his pride.
The small creatures worms and things
Which come out at a late hour
The big graceful owl his wings still spread out wide
Will shortly after devour.

Victoria Spray (10) St Modwens RC Primary School, Burton-On-Trent

THE MIGHTY SLIDE

The snow has fallen in the night
The temperature's exactly right
There goes Snowy down the slide
Followed by Bobtail and Frostie
Whoosh! Yeah!
They all said
With the glittering snow just ahead.

Bobtail a rabbit
Snowy a cat
Frostie a Guinea-pig
Just like that
They all slid through the snow
It was fun.

Look there's Guinness
Hiding low
He's a cat but not like Snow

They all played on the slide
Whooshing and hushing on the ride.

Sarah Pajor (11) St Modwens RC Primary School, Burton-On-Trent

THE LION CUB

The lion cub lies on the ground
It plays upon a grassy mound
Its soft brown eyes are open wide
It stares up at the morning sky.

It finds it likes to pat the air
As if there were a butterfly there.
It watches all the things go by.
The monkeys and the birds that fly.

Then as the sun beats down on it.
Its golden fur shines out.
No doubt that it's the cutest thing
That ever played about.

It opens up its tiny mouth
Displays a row of shining teeth
It twists and turns upon the ground
And starts to roll around, around.

Then it stops
Its black nose sniffs the air
He must go back to the lion's lair
For he will find his mother there
Go back with him if you dare.

Jane Appleby (11) St Modwens RC Primary School, Burton-On-Trent

THE FAWN

The fawn's fur was soft, thin, brushed back and
Coloured like something shaded in.
His eyes were starry, dark, dull and wide,
His little white patches all over his side.
He quietly trunched through the long weedy grass.
A forest of trees he will gently pass.

Rachel Ward (11) St Modwens RC Primary School, Burton-On-Trent

THE MIGHTY SLIDE

The snow has fallen in the night
The temperature is exactly right
It has fallen from a mighty height
And covered the playground in icy white.

Tricky Dicky, Dennis Dunn all waiting to have their
Fun
Child by child waiting to have their turn on
A mighty run.

Jo, Jane and Jack all waiting for a mighty smack
The teacher's coming round the bend, to see
The mighty slide in end.

The slide starts to melt away
The children start to fade away
The whistle goes the bell sounds too
In we go, our fingers blue.

Thomas Elliott (10) St Modwens RC Primary School, Burton-On-Trent

THE TIGER

The tiger has eyes as brown as mud
Glowing in the night.
  His teeth are white as snow.
He prowls around at night hunting for his food.
  He pounces like a kangaroo
But he never loses his lunch
  He moves swiftly along the grass.

Teresa Whittaker (11) St Modwens RC Primary School, Burton-On-Trent

SNOW TIME

The snow has fallen in the night
The children are jumping with delight,
The playground waiting for the children to come,
The children are coming to have their fun.

The first to arrive is Vicky Spray,
She slid across the ice and had a good play,
She, Dan and Fran are the best,
They are better than all the rest.

The last to arrive is Carla Roach,
She is a big slow coach,
She doesn't enjoy sliding across the ice,
Because she always wants to look nice.

When we were just starting, having our fun,
Sir came out and we got done,
Teachers never like to play,
That's what all of us like to say.

Frances Geoghegan (11) St Modwens RC Primary School,
                            Burton-On-Trent

THE ALLIGATOR

The alligator's scaly skin,
His teeth are shaped just like a pin,
He waits for his prey with his mouth open wide,
Searching and looking with his small beady eyes.

When he's in water he moves with a rapid pace,
But then on land it's a different case,
Moving slowly and swiftly along the land,
Making swirls of dust, kicking in the sand.

He's hunted down for his leathery skin,
It rubs along the ground as he sneakily
Races out of the water then back in,
Camouflaged in the water he lay,
Waiting for the first of his prey.

In the water he looks like an old rotten log,
Which you can just see through the misty fog,
He's waiting to pounce on a tortoise,
That he will crush between his jaws.

Daniela Todaro (11) St Modwens RC Primary School, Burton-On-Trent

THE BLACKBIRD

The blackbird sits on the tree,
as he looks for his tea.
He flaps his wings,
and learns to sing.
He beats his chest,
to get his breath.
The blackbird's yellow feet
dances with a treat.

Joshua Brian (10) St Peters CE Primary School, Caverswall

AUTUMN COLOURS

Autumn leaves of gold and gay,
In autumn the leaves fall every day,
Their red, orange and brown,
All the leaves fall down.

In the morning dew,
I may not see you.
With all the fog,
The nights get darker
When the clocks go back
There's a dog called Barker
Oh why, oh why,
Did the clocks go back.

Amy Jenkinson (10) St Peters CE Primary School, Caverswall

THE LION

Here comes the proud lion in the jungle,
He is the king all animals respect.
His mane so golden, shining in the sun.
Look how he hunts,
See him pounce.
I sure wish I was a lion.

He lives in a den,
It is his secret place,
He hears the monkey scream
The hunters are coming
He hides in the long long grass.

Fraser Greer (10) St Peters CE Primary School, Caverswall

WINTER TREES

The frost is stuck upon the walls,
The gentle wind sways against the trees.
August is gone and winter has arrived.
The leaves fall in the gale.
This is the start of my winter's tale.

The snow falls from the sky,
On top of trees and under leaves,
The bears crawl into their caves.
To hibernate for another day.
There is snow on the branches come and see,
Yes, I'm talking about you and me.

This is the last of my winter's tale.
I hope I see you not in the gale.
I think winter is the best,
Let's say goodbye to Robin's red breast
Now you've heard of all the gale
That's the end of my winter's tale.

Gavin Lake (10) St Peters CE Primary School, Caverswall

NATURE

The green woods
Flowering buds.
The nice view
The cows go moo!

Peaceful roads,
Water for toads,
The cockerel in the farmhouse,
Trying to catch the wood louse.

The blue sky
Where birds like to fly
Foxes run when there's no sun
Squirrels play all day,
Every duck should have some luck.

Slugs and snails
Make little trails
The trees have some bees
The nettles are green like you have seen
The long grass that we pass.

Samantha Brian (10) St Peters CE Primary School, Caverswall

SPRINGY THINGS

There are lots of springy things in the world,
Like daffodils, snowdrops, green trees and birds,
They all appear when winter goes away,
Spring must take his place for
Winter needs a holiday,
Eggs we all get are made of chocolate not shell,
A rabbit wakes early to deliver them well.

There are lots of springy things in the world,
Like daffodils, snowdrops, green trees and birds,
The insects get busy while butterflies flutter by,
Birds in the tree tops sing their melody,
Birds and bugs are both springy things,
And in the season of warmth they are flapping their wings.

There are lots of springy things in the world,
Like daffodils, snowdrops, green trees and birds,
Now I must mention the plant life you'll see,
Green leaves on the trees unseen until February,
Buds will soon blossom and flowers you will see
But the blooms will come when summer it will be.

Thomas Copeland (10) St Peters CE Primary School, Caverswall

WHAT HELD YOU UP THIS TIME SPRING?

What took you so long spring?
Why didn't you bring the daffodils earlier?
Why were the birds so late?
What happened to you with your wispy white clouds
Was your train late,
Why, oh why were you late!

You could have come earlier
Instead of leaving us cold,
Why couldn't you come
What happened to the lovely bright sun.
We were desperate for your gentle breezes
And the birds making their nests.

Thank goodness you came along at all
With all your beauties,
And all your bright flowers
Shining in your warm blazing sun,
With your clear blue sky with specks of cloud,
Thank goodness you bothered to come.

John Buttanshaw (10) St Peters CE Primary School, Caverswall

THE BLACKBIRD

The blackbird has a yellow beak,
On a bleak and misty week.
Shiny feathers made like leathers
In the bleak and misty weather.
Fluffy wings that ring and ding
In the spring they sing.
Yellow feet that beat the seat,
That makes me want to meet.

Sits on a tree with tea for three,
That makes me laugh with glee.
Yellow beaks that also speak,
So I go for a peek.
Yellow feet that beat
So I give them a treat.
Their fluffy wings that sing,
Makes me feel like spring.

Helene Balewski (10) St Peters CE Primary School, Caverswall

THE EARTH IS ROUND

The Earth is round bigger than a pound.
Humans look up into space,
I couldn't see anything apart from
My father's face.

Everybody uses the Earth as a bin,
On the floor go the bottles of gin,
Empty space covered is stars,
I feel like I've eaten the planet Mars.

Arriving home I see the clouds moving,
I really feel like grooving.
Round the sun the Earth spins,
It feels like it's hanging on by pins.

Tins of baked beans for my tea
It's good they can be recycled.
I wish I could be.

Hurry hurry the Earth spins round
People used to think it
Wasn't round.

Hannah Wilson & Hannah Thomas (10) St Peters CE Primary
School, Caverswall

WINTER TREES

All the trees are bare,
No-one seems to care.
So what do they wear.
They stand in the air
Each branch will swing
to the sound of the wind.

Ice on the trees,
Bare branch with no leaves
Thick and thin branches see,
I like the way it looks at me,
When the cold breezes go around.

Pine trees are spiky.
Fur trees are soft
We've got a million trees
Up in the loft.

Jason Hawkes (10) St Peters CE Primary School, Caverswall

WHAT IS LIFE?

I just sat there wondering
What life was all about.
What was the meaning of this.
All we do is live and die.
Everyday wondering why
We just live like this.
In a world of wars and drugs.
Why do it?
All it does is make it worse.
After all,
What is life really like?

Kira Dable (11) Silverdale CP School

124

NATURE

I like nature with plants and great big trees.
I like animals from elephants down to fleas.
I would like to save the forests that
are always being cut down.
I would like to know how fish stay
Under the water but never drown.
I would like to grow a triffid so the
Plants could fight back.
I would like to see a zebra with stripes
All down its back.
I would like to know more to be able
To save the Earth.
I would like more people to listen but
I'm only eleven for what it's worth.

Ian Glover (11) Silverdale CP School

WINNING THE RACE

When I won the race
I was really glad.
I got the gold medal
And the other people
Were really mad.
I ran as hard as
I could and
Trained as hard as
I could.
And all the people
Cheered for me
And helped me to
The end.

Rachel Heath (9) Silverdale CP School

AT THE ZOO

There was a man with three toes,
Who went to the zoo with a hose,
He blew up the birds,
They came out in herds,
And a parrot got stuck up his nose.

Samantha Gilford (10) Silverdale CP School

FOOLS

There was a time when days were black
When serpents raged the stormy seas and
dragons flew in the mountain breeze
they instantly fell upon any fools who dared
to play the weekly pools.

Timothy O'Neill (10) Silverdale CP School

SEE THEM GO

See them go through the air,
Zooming, booming, flashing by,
Up, down, round and round,
Making patterns red, white and blue,
That is the Red Arrows for you.

Amy Robinson (10) Silverdale CP School

126

WINTER'S DAY

Blowing beautiful crystal white
The snow is falling into the night
Trying to warm my tingly toes
Perishing as the wind blows
The sky was grey with patches of blue
And then the sun came shining through.

Gregory Barlow (10) Silverdale CP School

SAVE OUR EARTH

Pollution, litter everywhere
Dirtying the ground and all the air
Animals' lives are put at risk
Why don't people think about this?

Tin cans, bottles and wrappers from sweets
You can see as you walk down the street.
Forests destroyed and trees cut down,
That's enough to make me frown.

But you can help, it's not too late,
Give our world a brighter fate.
So come on everyone, use your brains,
Work together and achieve this aim!

I wrote this poem for my Mum
A message for everyone.
It would be better if we tried
To help animals instead of them losing their lives.

Elizabeth Williamson (9) The Close Junior School

PEOPLE

Amy is angry
Charlotte is shameless
David is daft,
Makes everyone laugh.
Emma is exciting
Faye is funny
Gareth is gloomy
Heather is hungry
And Jessica is me
Just wait and see,
Jessica is jolly.
Kalvir is kicking a ball
Lorna never plays at all
Matthew is a monkey
Nicky is jumpy
Peter rides a pony
Ricky's very lonely
Sam is silly
Tim plays with Billy
Donna is clever
Mark found a feather.

Jessica Stephenson (8) The Close Junior School

A SECRET PLACE

Newts crawl in unknown places,
We lift the stones to find them.
Slithering slugs,
Burrowing worms,
Colourful snails -
All hiding from birds.

Tadpoles swim,
Frogs croak,
Centipedes, spiders and beetles
Scurry away,
As we approach.
Ladybirds eating tiny mites.

Now I know where to find them!

Alicia Hibberts (10) The Faber RC Primary School

A PEACEFUL PLACE

As we trod,
We watched our step.
The grass was long,
The soil was wet.

As I watched
A newt go by,
I saw a robin
In the sky.

I watched a spider
Spin its web,
For insects that
Would soon be dead.

The web, like silk,
And, oh, so fine!
The glittering sun
Did make it shine!

A peaceful place,
And undisturbed.
The sound of birds
Was all I heard.

Vanessa Rowlinson (10) The Faber RC Primary School

THE DESERTED GARDEN

We trod very carefully
through piercing brambles and
massive docks,
Amidst long, soft, waving grasses.
An ornamental pond
in the middle of the ground,
Where newts, orange and brown,
with wriggling bodies, long and smooth,
Hide under the rocks.
Ladybirds,
black spotted, tiny creatures
Eating aphids, on the leaves.

Thomas Shenton (8) The Faber RC Primary School

THE HIDDEN GARDEN

We trod carefully
Underneath the overhanging trees.
Our legs were scratched by the
piercing brambles.
Bushes around us,
thick and dense.
Sharp, stinging nettles, giving pain.
Newts, hiding under stones.
Beetles, scuttling over stones.
Black, spotted ladybirds, eating aphids.
Snails, crawling in the shade.
Bindweed, strangling smaller plants.
Worms, wriggling free from their holes.
Bright, yellow buttercups, gleaming in the sun.
Purple-headed thistles, attracting hovering bees.
This peaceful garden, hiding many secrets.

James Hall (9) The Faber RC Primary School

THE WASTE GARDEN

We trod carefully
Along the grassy floor.
We saw newts
Sliding, in the muddy ground,
Then hiding,
Under rocks and stones.
We saw trees -
Like holly, elder and pine.
Long slugs,
As black as night.
Scurrying spiders.
Hiding in cracks.
Long grass,
Tickling my legs.
Rows
of plants,
Waving their heads.

Thomas Bishop (9) The Faber RC Primary School

THE SECRET GARDEN

As we trod carefully
through the undisturbed ground.
We felt the long grass -
tickling our legs.
Clinging ivy, was growing -
up the tall trees.
I saw a spider -
spinning its silky web.
Then flowers made me sneeze,
So I had to hide,
Under the old ash tree,
at the side.

Victoria Brindley (10) The Faber RC Primary School

THE FORGOTTEN GARDEN

Caterpillars curling
In the overgrown grass,
While the little children pass.
Behind the rock,
There was a newt,
Eating a piece of root.
Newts, brown and orange,
Creeping by.
Trees overhanging from on high.

Thin green leaves,
Tadpoles with plump tails,
Snails with colourful shells,
Long, yellow buttercups,
Bluebells, royal and blue.

We trotted carefully,
Across the long, tickling grass.
Quiet,
Not to disturb the living creatures.

Rosanna Rowlinson (9) The Faber RC Primary School

A SECRET GARDEN

As I entered an undisturbed garden,
I saw a butterfly, give his pardon.
I saw two tadpoles in the pond,
And one little newt, of whom I grew fond.
Docks with huge leaves,
Small ants in teams.
Shrubs with pink flowers,
Trees with great boughs.
Now I must go,
Before the wind starts to blow.

Lorna Gould (10) The Faber RC Primary School

THE RIVER

I see the river slowly drifting by,
The sun blazing down,
On its rippled surface.

I see the bulrushes,
Swaying in the wind,
The ducks going past,
With their ducklings.

I faintly see the fishes,
Swimming under the water,
So when you're walking past a river,
Stop and take a look.

Samantha Hatton (11) Park Primary School

NOTHING

The page is blank,
There's nothing to do,
There's no-one to thank,
And the tank's gone too.

              You can run in.
              And you can run out.
              Whatever made nothing must
              be a sin,
              Wherever you go when,
              out and about,
              You can always see
              something that is or is not!

Natalie Arrowsmith (11) Park Primary School

LONELINESS

I hate feeling lonely,
It makes me feel sad,
You lose your trust,
You want to hide,
And you feel scared.
There's no-one you can talk to,
You feel really bad,
You want to be alone,
'Cause no-one understands.
So the best thing to do,
Is to phone your grandparents,
Because kind words are their only language.
So the next time you feel this feeling,
Just go and use the phone,
And don't worry what to say,
Just say 'I feel alone!'

Amy Langford (11) Park Primary School

DARKNESS

The moon was shining in a sea of black,
Above the old man who sleeps in a sack.
His legs are bent, arthritic with work,
And he eats and sleeps, lives in dirt.

The night brings peace and quiet to his life,
Just one long struggle to stay alive.
He no longer cares where he lives or how,
Long forgotten his struggle to reach for power.
He lies alone, no package of things,
And waits to see what morning brings.

Emma Rigby (11) Park Primary School

CARDBOARD CITY

Cardboard city
What a big city.
No houses on the streets
Just cardboard boxes.
So warm in summer,
So cold in winter.
The doors are our blankets;
In the alleyways, our neighbours are
stray cats and dogs.
What a place - and remember the
phrase -
'Cardboard City' -
Because anyone can get in here
But not many get out.

Lindsey Pullin (11) Park Primary School

WEATHER MAKES ME FEEL

When it rains I feel dull and lazy like a slow tortoise
When the sun shines I feel happy and bright like
dolphins jumping in and out of the sea.
When the snow glitters I feel active as if
I want to go sledging like a whizzing roller coaster ride.
When it's cloudy I feel cold and shivery just like
a polar bear without any fur in the North Pole.
When it hails it hits me hard on the head like a
hammer knocking a nail into wood.

Victoria Pople (9) Park Primary School

PIGS

Pigs are pink and round and fat,
With curly tails and a nose that's flat,
You'll find them snuffling in the ground,
And rolling in mud round and round -
In their sties they sleep away,
Waiting for another piggy day.

Caroline Wall (11) Park Primary School

RIVERS

Rivers are blue
Rivers are green
Rivers are all over the place.
From the tops of hills
Under bridges
Past the town
And the villages.

Matthew Lloyd (8) Park Primary School

DARKNESS

As black as a witch's hat
As black as storm clouds
As black as a pair of boots
As black as the switched off TV screen
As black as a cat
As black as the pupil of your eye
As black as everything when you are blind.

Heidi Thacker (8) Park Primary School

THE HAUNTED HOUSE

Once there was a house
Where many people lived
And soon they died
And everyone cried
And soon it was forgotten
A person went to see
What the house could be
And when he came back
He was as pale as a ghost.
The people asked what happened
But all they could get
Was a little mutter.
The people waited till he was right
And they asked if he had a fright
People never went a step to the house
Because the house was haunted.

Nicola Williams (9) Park Primary School

WEATHER

The weather is gloomy, dull and grey,
I like the hot summer sun on a warm day,
The brightest yellow, orange and red,
But now it's all gloomy, dull and wet.

Hurry hurry tomorrow come
Let the sunny colours come
Make this month of June be bright
Make the rain get out of sight.

Hannah Spencer (9) Park Primary School

SISTER SISTER

sister sister let me play
sister sister go away
sister sister give me a book
sister sister I'm good luck
sister sister I'm with you
sister sister I love you

Nicola Pegg (10) Park Primary School

THE MAGICAL ERASER

My friend's name is Ian.
I told him about my magical eraser.
He took no notice so I told him again.
He did listen.
He said, 'No, you have not.'
I said, 'Yes I have and I will prove it.'
So I erased him.

Daniel Warner (8) Park Primary School

I FOUND SOMETHING HAIRY!

I found something hairy down by the loo!
It was purple, pink and spotted -
I didn't know what to do.
Put it in the bath tub?
Put it in the sink? -
Flush it down the toilet!
Now - it's black and pink!

Nicholas Gregory (11) Park Primary School

GHOSTS (AND A BIT ABOUT JULIAN CLAREY!)

Goulish ghosts are in my house
Haunting us and teasing my mouse.
Oscar's his name - he told my Mom,
Mary.
Scary is Oscar to my Mom, Mary.
Teasing and terrifying!
As bad as Julian Clarey!
Screaming the house down
Is my Mom, Mary,
While she's watching Julian Clarey!

Dominic Pitt (8) Park Primary School

SEASHORE

Sun shines bright with the blazing light.
The sun glitters along the waves.
The water washes the shore.
It's a time not to ignore.
Water is cold.
When running in the sea it seems to fold.
The seagulls fly over the rocks.
The seagulls are full with delight
to know that it is nearly night
and they always seem to be right.
Now the day is nearly done
there won't be any sun.
Now there is thunder and lightning
and the thunder sounds like a blasting gun.

Craig Ball (11) Park Primary School

THE LAST MONSTER

I used to be fearsome and bold
But now I am scared of people
So don't kill me.
I am the last monster.
I won't hurt you so don't hurt me.
I will collect everything you need
I will keep you from danger
If you keep me away from danger.
I will care for you.

Paul Brookes (8) Park Primary School

THE GLEN

The glen just glooms
Just lying sad and gloomy.
But then an eagle glides over
And wakes the glen up
From its gloomy dinginess.
This made it very angry
A rumble could be heard under the ground.
Then a stagnant pool started to ripple
The drops from the clouds are now stones.
Then a thin strip of yellow fire hits the glen.
Then with a sudden boom it goes quiet
again just as though that the angry glen
had never got angry.
Then the glen was back to its normal
dingy gloomy self again.

Michael Rigby (9) Park Primary School

COLD

It was a cold winter's day,
I opened the curtains, it was snowing.
I rushed to get my clothes on
I shot downstairs
I hurried eating my breakfast
I ran outside
These people were having a snowball fight
I joined in
I got soaked to the bone
It was time for lunch.
I had already got my fourth set of clothes on
I went sledding and smashed my sledge up the wall.
I carried it home.
It was time for bed.
The next morning I woke up,
opened the curtains it was sunny
and all of the snow had gone.

Neil Birch (11) Park Primary School

GUESS WHO?

He's got muscles like rock
He's as strong as ten men
He stands as a sky scraper
He's as famous as Sylvester Stalone
His muscles pop out like balloons
I'll be back he says in his great movies
He could pick up a ton
He weighs about 20 stone
Can you guess?
      Arnold S

Ashley Lawton (10) Park Primary School

THE DAMSEL FLY

I'm a dazzling damsel fly
Dazzling delectably, dancing free.
This delicate dancing damsel fly.
Is me!

Hayley Stanton (9) Walhouse CE Junior School

NOTHING BUT NONSENSE

I'm a frisky little water flea,
Fast and furious that's like me,
Fantastic with fashion,
Just a tiny fury fish,
Said he,
A microscopic wonder of the pond,
If you wish.

Christian Bury (9) Walhouse CE Junior School

THE BORING BEETLE

Wiggling, whirling, wondering -
Wondering what to do.
A whirligig beetle is a very dull thing
And so is its life too.

Richard Meads (8) Walhouse CE Junior School

THE DANCING DAMSEL FLY

I'm a dazzling, decorative, damsel fly,
Playing all day, while the time goes by,
'Til the red sun sets
Slowly in the west.
I sleep when it's dark,
I'm up again with the lark,
To dance my dizzy dance.

Oliver Lawton Poxon : Walhouse CE Junior School

WATER FLEA

I'm a wondrous wondering water flea,
I love the pond!
I feel so free,
I'm transparent as can be.
I'm a fantastic, fragile water flea!

Carly Fijalkowski (9) Walhouse CE Junior School

THE SWAN CHORUS

King and Queen of the swans we;
No other birds so grand we see!
None but we have feathers like snow!
With orange bright beaks
and eyes aglow,
Pluskin; pluskin, swany jee!
We think no swan so happy as we!
Splashkin, splashkin, swans jill!
We think so then, and we thought so still!

Louise Foster (9) Walhouse CE Junior School

THE KINGFISHER CHORUS

King and Queen of the kingfisher we;
No other bird so grand we see!
None but we have feathers like parrots!
With blue, orange, white and black!
Kloshkin, klishkin, kingfisher jee!
We think no birds so happy as we!
Fishy, floshy, flashy jill!
We think so then, and we thought so still!

Kayleigh Evans (9) Walhouse CE Junior School

THE WOMAN

A woman stood and stared at me,
Or was it me she was staring at?

I looked into her eyes,
They were balls of fire, rings of gold, lashes of silver
At first they seemed evil, but then lost, scared, alone.
The woman touched me, I'm sure she did,
But nothing moved, not one muscle.
I wanted to run, run far away, but my feet seemed
Nailed firmly into the ground.
Why did I walk to her? I felt as though I was
Being controlled by her glare - hypnotised.
Someone was trying to reach me.
I finally escaped, was set free into a
Different world.

A woman stood and stared at me.
Or was it me she was staring at?

Adele Bates (11) William Hutson Junior School

SPIDER

It was just sitting there,
Harmless and still
I won't kill it
But if it moves I sure will.

I'll just go over
And turn on the tap
If it doesn't stay still
It's gonna go splat.

What if it slips
And falls down the drain?
What if it's never
To be seen again?

Poor little spider
Its legs are elastic
I go pick it up
And see that it's plastic.

Nicola Cox (11) William Hutson Junior School

INFORMATION

We hope you have enjoyed reading this book - and that you will continue to enjoy it in the coming years.

If you like reading and writing poetry drop us a line, or give us a call, and we'll send you a free information pack.

Write to

Young Writers Information
1-2 Wainman Road
Woodston
Peterborough
PE2 7BU